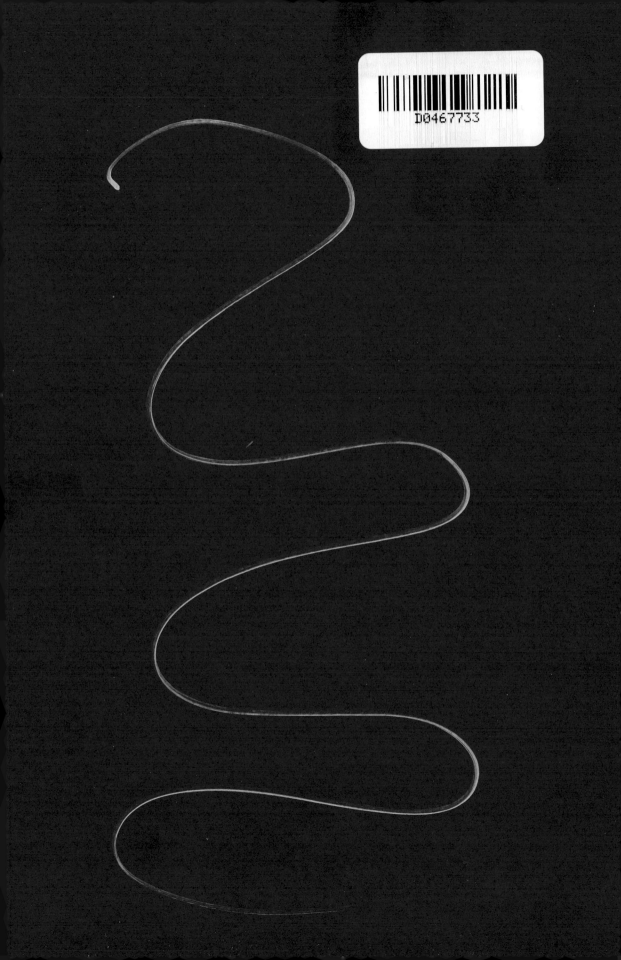

FANTASTIC FUGITIVES

CRIMINALS, CUTTHROATS, AND REBELS WHO

CHANGED HISTORY

WHILE ON THE RUN

WITHDRAWN

BRIANNA DUMONT

Sky Pony Press
NEW YORK

ALSO BY BRIANNA DUMONT:

Famous Phonies: Legends, Fakes, and Frauds Who Changed History

Sky Pony Press books may be purchased in bulk at special discounts for sales promotion, corporate gifts, fund-raising, or educational purposes. Special editions can also be created to specifications. For details, contact the Special Sales Department, Sky Pony Press, 307 West 36th Street, 11th Floor, New York, NY 10018 or info@skyhorsepublishing.com.

Sky Pony® is a registered trademark of Skyhorse Publishing, Inc.®, a Delaware corporation.

Visit our website at www.skyponypress.com.

10 9 8 7 6 5 4 3 2 1

Manufactured in China, September 2015
This product conforms to CPSIA 2008

Library of Congress Cataloging-in-Publication Data is available on file.

Cover design by Sarah Brody and Brian Peterson
Front cover photo credit Shutterstock; back cover photo credit Wikimedia Commons
Interior illustrations by Bethany Straker
Book design by Sara Kitchen

Print ISBN: 978-1-63220-412-7
Ebook ISBN: 978-1-63450-932-9

Contents

Author's Note

This book isn't your typical history book. It's not about names, dates, and battles. Sure, those are all in here, but at the heart of this book is my best attempt to make history come alive through the real people who made it happen. To that end, you won't find any pesky footnotes or highfalutin arguments that belong to scholars. (That stuff is in back of the book, where it's not as fun.) Here, it's all about the stories. If you find one that speaks to your soul, there's plenty of further reading and research material to explore in the Sources and Notes on Sources.

And whatever you do, don't expect ho-hum, dusty-as-the-Sahara retellings of these fantastic fugitives. Their lives weren't boring, so their stories shouldn't be, either. Buckle up for all kinds of rowdy misbehavior told with a healthy dose of sarcasm. When you're on the run, life is bound to get bumpy.

enter at your own risk

Introduction

Caution: "Bad" Is All about Perspective

If you're going to change the world, you better be good at running and hiding. That's because change doesn't come easily. Those in power usually like things the way they are. It's no surprise, really, since they get to enjoy the benefits. If you rock the boat, they won't be happy. They may even want your head. But don't let that stop you. As you'll see from these stories, even on the run, you can still leave your mark.

Not every fugitive is running from the police. Kings, countries, and churches have been known to put a price on someone's head, and you'll find plenty of political and religious fugitives in this book, too.

Because fugitives need secrecy to stay alive, it's not always easy to know all the details of their exploits. Don't worry; these stories aren't embellished willy-nilly. Every fantastic detail is 100 percent true. Or at least as far as we know. Being on the run doesn't leave a lot of time for memoir writing unless you're caught and thrown in the slammer like a few of our rebels.

Some of the fugitives you'll encounter in this book are easy to root for because they fight the forces of evil, but even heroes have a wart or two. Everyone is human, which means everyone makes mistakes. Still, all of the fugitives were fantastic in one way or another. Some were fantastic people you might want to grab a milkshake with while others have hard-to-believe fantastical stories. Although not all of them were great people, their bad behavior made good change happen.

Just like them, *you* can change history. Stand up for what you believe in and don't be afraid to make the world a better place; just make sure you have your running shoes tied tight.

Spartacus

The Low-Aiming Freedom Fighter

Rome Wasn't Built in a Day, but It *Was* Built on the Backs of Slaves

Spartacus could have been *the* heartthrob pinup of his day. He had good looks, hunky arms, and that X factor that made everyone in the room need smelling salts. The Romans saw it and made the slave a gladiator. They trained him to be a ruthless death-dealing warrior, but for some reason it shocked them when he turned on them next.

Before Spartacus bit the hand that fed him, revolt was already in the air. Thanks to two previous slave uprisings, unrest wafted around Italy as contagious as the flu. Being a Roman slave was hard work, and the slaves were sick and tired of man-powering the world's biggest bully—the **empire of Rome**.

empire of Rome:

Hold on—wasn't Rome a republic during Spartacus's revolt? Technically, yes. The first emperor didn't take over the marble throne until 27 BCE, partially thanks to Spartacus, but the Roman Republic was arguably an empire before that. It had a unified government, always looked to its neighbors for more land, and had amphitheaters full of different peoples under their rule.

Being a gladiator meant being desirable, deadly, and disgusting all at once to the Roman elite. Watching grown men duke it out to the bloody end was a favorite pastime of Roman citizens. That part didn't really bother Spartacus. Blood games and fights to the death were totally normal in the first century BCE. He just didn't like being the one on the sharp end of a sword every day.

A Puzzle of a Guy

Who knows when Spartacus was born; it wasn't like he was supposed to grow up and be famous. It was somewhere in **Thrace** during the Roman Republic, a time in which a bunch of old, wrinkly guys in Rome called a Senate ruled over the population. The Senate was known for doing things like ordering legions of men to go conquer other people and bring them back lots of slaves and gold.

Thrace:
Present-day Bulgaria.

Thracians were known for fighting with abandon, spearing men's heads and screaming like crazy when they attacked their enemies. Let's just say no self-respecting Roman citizen wanted to meet a Thracian in a dark alley. The Senate realized the ferocious Thracians would make good Roman soldiers, but they didn't want to actually make them real Roman soldiers. Instead, the senators hired Thracians to fight in **auxiliary** units on the Roman side, but not in the legions. Those were for Roman citizens only.

auxiliary:
Literally the "help." Auxiliaries were not native Romans, and they got about a third of the pay that Roman legionaries did. They provided manpower and specialized fighting techniques like horseback riding.

Spartacus was a free Thracian who fought in a Roman auxiliary, but he didn't stay for long. He deserted and was caught, which was bad news if he ever wanted to go home again. The price for desertion from a Roman auxiliary unit was slavery. Since Spartacus was a hunk in leather armor and muscled like a WWE wrestler, he was sold to a gladiator school. These

schools were all around Roman Europe, but Spartacus was sold to one in Capua, near Pompeii.

schools:

You're probably thinking of the Colosseum in Rome at this point. Don't. It won't be built for another 140 years. Games were held in amphitheaters that looked a lot like the oval Colosseum, though.

It could have been worse. Slaves in Rome were considered tools—expensive ones who ate, slept, and pooped, but on the same level as a hammer. They were frequently sold to work the fields, to build public projects, or to mine for gold all day. All this was done to build and glorify Rome. Gladiators, on the other hand, ate like kings and had top-notch doctors for any boo-boos they got in training. If a gladiator survived his first season, not only was he lucky, he'd soon be seeing the three Gs: gold, girls, and glory.

That doesn't mean being a gladiator was a great gig. Many gladiators didn't survive long enough to become hyped-up celebrities, chased and harassed by adoring fans.

In addition to military deserters, gladiators were also picked from the worst kinds of criminals. This didn't exactly make for a homey atmosphere in the shared barracks, but it was perfect for bloodthirsty games.

Spartacus wasn't chosen to become a gladiator simply because he was all muscles and tired of marching. He also had that "it" quality, which made people drool.

That "it" factor made him an awesome gladiator, but it also made him dangerous to Rome. When Spartacus talked about escape during lunchtime or before bed, people listened.

The original Hulk: a Thracian.

Are you blind, Ref? His toe was over the line!

The Thracians were into his plan because Spartacus was blood, and the **Gauls** were into it because they liked blood.

Gauls:

Known for fighting naked and to the death, and their women were known for stabbing their own men if they fled a battle.

The Gauls voted in their own co-leader, Crixus the Gaul, and Spartacus and his new BFF, Crixus, decided all they had to do was overpower the puny guards and run like heck for the mountains. They were prime-time killing machines; what could go wrong?

It didn't bother Spartacus and Crixus when all they could find for weapons were kitchen skewers and pots and pans. Seventy slaves fought their way out, and they didn't look back. Just a few miles down the road,

Spartacus and his crew seized a wagon full of weapons and exchanged their forks for swords.

Now they could hightail it home to Thrace and forget all this slave business ever happened. They could raise some sheep or farm a bunch of wheat. From here on, they'd only kill for their own fun, not for some snooty senator's weekend pleasure. Maybe that's all that Spartacus really wanted. As for the rest of the fugitives, living well wasn't exactly the sort of revenge they had in mind.

"Living Well Is the Best Revenge" Is *So* Overrated

What's the first thing a fugitive needs if he hopes to remain undetected? A really awesome hiding spot, of course. Spartacus and his **men** chose Mount Vesuvius—the volcano—as their ideal hiding place. Don't worry, it still had another 152 years to go before the **Big One**. In 73 BCE, Vesuvius was a fugitive's paradise. It had all the fertile farmland, runaway farm slaves, and rich farmhouse villas for plundering that a ragtag army could want. The local slaves flocked to Spartacus like togas to an amphitheater when he arrived.

When Rome heard about the escapees, the Senate didn't get too worked up about it. Runaways were hardly worth interrupting their daily parties. They had to do something, though, so they sent in a rookie. Gaius Claudius Glaber wasn't a somebody; all the somebodies were busy fighting real battles against barbarians and bringing honor to their names. Fighting slaves wasn't honorable, but someone had to put an end to these slaves' freedom. Glaber got three thousand men and strict instruc-

men:
And an unknown number of women and children, too. We know Spartacus definitely brought his lady friend along, but we don't know her name.

Big One:
Mount Vesuvius blew its top in 79 CE, covering the towns of Pompeii and Herculaneum in a thick layer of ash. While not a great situation for all the people living there, it's really great for archaeologists today who can study a perfectly preserved Roman town.

Fawning Fan Club
or Jealous Haters?

Before Banksy, there were the Romans. Let's face it, everyone loves to graffiti. Ancient Pompeii, being preserved under ash, has some of the best examples of this ancient art form. The graffiti at Pompeii includes little jewels of insight chiseled all over the city, including the gladiatorial barracks where men lived, slept, and ate together. Here are some gladiators who left their mark more literally:

- *Celadus the Thracian: The heartthrob who made all the girls swoon.*
- *Marcus Attilius: The rookie who bested two champions.*
- *Antiochus: The guy who got to hang there with his girl, Cithera.*
- *Jesus: The non-famous dude who ribbed the gladiator Lucius Asicius for smelling like fish sauce—the cheap kind.*

tions to make it quick before things got embarrassing.

Like a dummy, Glaber thought he could rely on his superior Roman brain to win against Spartacus and his band of escapees. Glaber decided to starve the runaways into submission by setting up camp at the foot of Mount Vesuvius to wait them out. Maybe he warmed up some goat milk and tucked into bed for the night. The next thing Glaber knew, Spartacus and his men were rappelling down the mountain using vines they had roped together. They slaughtered many of Glaber's men and plundered his camp after the rest fled. It was a mortifying defeat, even for a rookie.

Still, Rome wasn't too worried. Until Spartacus beat the next army sent by Rome to defeat them, and the next one after that. The senators were starting to get a little hot under their togas, but they didn't barricade themselves in an arrow-proof bunker yet. After all, the gladiators were merely runaway slaves.

The senators had a big problem, though. The slaves were starting to attract a huge following, and we're not talking about Twitter.

Practically Ghandi with a Sword

Unlike Glaber and the Romans, Spartacus didn't underestimate his enemy. He fought as ferociously and craftily as a Thracian, but, thanks to his time as an auxiliary soldier, he also knew Roman military tactics. Soon, thousands of

Barbarians beat us Roman legionaries? Doubtful.

frustrated freemen and overworked slaves had joined Spartacus's open rebellion. The men trained by day and plundered by night.

It wasn't all fun and games. Serious differences came between BFFs Crixus and Spartacus. Crixus wanted more loot and more war. Spartacus wanted to go home to Thrace, but as we know from the Odyssey, getting home isn't always easy in the ancient world. They patched up their argument for the time being and decided to stay in Italy, fighting the armies Rome kept slinging at them.

For the senators, it wasn't any fun and games. They sent another army and another army to chase down the fugitives, but it wasn't easy finding them.

Spartacus knew he couldn't beat the Romans in a fair fight, so he played dirty. He preferred hit-and-run tactics where he and his band could taunt the enemy rather than getting mowed down on some open field.

Spartacus marched up and down Italy like he owned the place, freeing slaves, foraging in people's houses for food, and gaining support—like forty thousand people sort of support. When his band looted, Spartacus divided the spoils evenly. Since even freemen got in on the action, Spartacus must have been pretty persuasive. Now it was time to go home to Thrace in triumph.

Too bad Crixus didn't see it the same way. To him and the ten thousand fellow fugitives he persuaded, the Romans hadn't paid enough for their behavior, and the only currency Crixus would accept was blood. Spartacus parted ways for good and went north, taking the thirty thousand rebels he'd collected from the countryside with him.

If Crixus's main goal was killing Romans, he accomplished it easily. If his second goal was to stay alive, he failed dismally. It wasn't because the Roman generals had gotten wise to the rebels' guerilla-style tricks; it was because Crixus was no Spartacus. Discipline, scouting, tactics—all those things were for wimps. (Or, in this case, the living.)

Crixus went down in a blaze of glory, screaming like a naked hooligan and taking everyone in his path down with him. Spartacus was **on his own**.

on his own:

But he did take a day to honor Crixus by making a few captured Roman soldiers play gladiator against each other, which was totally degrading.

Good thing Spartacus was already heading home. Without his partner in crime, he was vulnerable. Yet, when Spartacus and his men reached the edge of the Alps, he turned around and marched back down Italy toward Sicily.

Say what? He finally made it to the Alps and then *turned around?* It wasn't because he loved sightseeing and slurping **pasta** with his woman. He was vetoed from continuing on to Thrace by his men. Maybe it was the Alps, with its snow and altitude sickness. Maybe it was because Spartacus never told his followers his real plan. (Or us.) Or maybe it was because those peeved ex-slaves really wanted to sack Rome itself. They were drunk on victory, which is never a good thing.

pasta:

Spaghetti and meatballs weren't around yet, and tomato sauce wasn't eaten in Italy until the eighteenth century. Imagine instead porridge, bread, and cheese for the masses, and for the really fancy folks, roasted parrots, flamingo tongues, and puppies.

A Gallic vs. Roman Smack-Down

Gauls and Romans were as different in their fighting styles as cotton candy and steel. Here's a rundown:

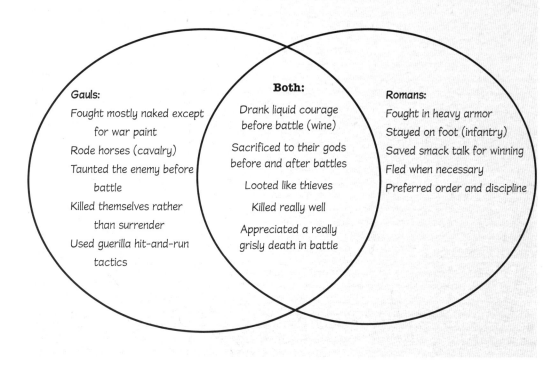

Gauls:

Fought mostly naked except for war paint

Rode horses (cavalry)

Taunted the enemy before battle

Killed themselves rather than surrender

Used guerilla hit-and-run tactics

Both:

Drank liquid courage before battle (wine)

Sacrificed to their gods before and after battles

Looted like thieves

Killed really well

Appreciated a really grisly death in battle

Romans:

Fought in heavy armor

Stayed on foot (infantry)

Saved smack talk for winning

Fled when necessary

Preferred order and discipline

Whatever the real reason, the fugitives busted a U-ey and marched back down Italy toward the capital.

It Takes Money

Like every good story, this one has a cringe-worthy antagonist. For Spartacus, it was Marcus Licinius Crassus. Crassus was a somebody in Rome. He got rich and powerful by helping people put out fires. If that sounds weird, that's because it is. Crassus ran a firefighting service, but he didn't offer it for free.

When a person's house caught on fire and slowly reduced to ashes, Crassus would negotiate for his "firefighter" services, which were really just a bunch of slaves with buckets of water. The longer the house burned, the more Crassus would demand in payment. Nothing personal, just business. After the house burned down, he'd negotiate a super-low rate to take the ruined property off the owner's hands. What a guy! Then again, his dad earned the nickname "he who does not laugh," so it's not surprising that ruthlessness ran in the family.

Mr. Scrooge (Crassus) became so rich off other people's misery that he could afford his own legions to hunt down Spartacus. If he could beat Spartacus, then he'd become popular enough in Rome to be elected **consul**. Crassus finagled four legions from the Senate and bought six more from his own coin purse. Fighting slaves may not have been honorable. Saving Rome, though . . . now, that was.

consul:

Two men were elected consul each year. Consuls were the most powerful men in Rome during the Republic and similar to a president today.

Crassus would need deep pockets to take down the former gladiator. Spartacus had treated Italy like his personal playground for almost two years, making Roman legions run away crying.

Crassus had about forty-five thousand legionaries to get the job done, which is the same number Julius Caesar took to conquer *all* of Gaul only a couple of decades later. Crassus clearly wasn't taking any chances. Although Spartacus had more men, they weren't trained killing machines like legionaries, just ticked off farmers with pitchforks.

Both men had a strategy for battle. Crassus planned to herd the former gladiator into a spikey dead end, trapping him between the sea and Crassus's legionaries. Spartacus relied on pirates that he'd bribe to sail him and his men to Sicily—and to safety. Why Spartacus thought pirates would ever keep their word is another question. In the end, the pirates took his gold and ran, leaving Spartacus crunched between the sea and the big ole wall that Crassus's men built.

Spartacus still had a lot of crazy Gauls among his followers, and once again, they decided to go out on their own—naked and screaming and fighting to the death.

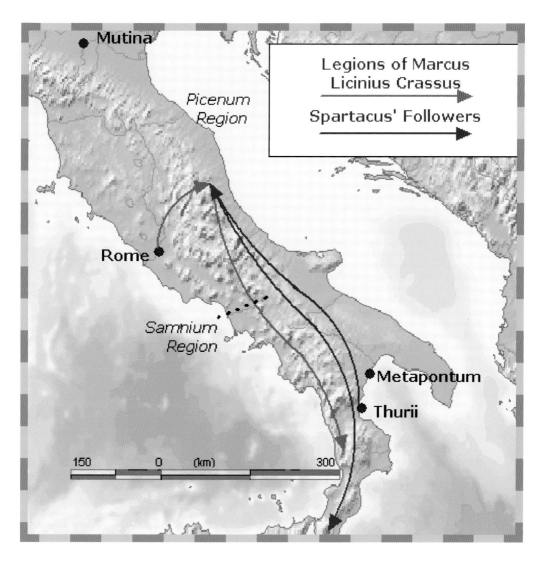

Home sweet Thrace—NOT.

Crassus out-generalled the Gauls and gave them exactly what they always wanted—a really gory death in battle.

And We've Come to the End

After the Gauls bit the dust, Spartacus's army shrunk faster than wool in a dryer, but he had another, bigger problem on his hands. The Roman senators were so scared of him by this point that they'd recalled some of the other somebodies from conquering land and people abroad. Things were only going to get worse for Spartacus.

The two sides lined up for battle, which is exactly the opposite of what Spartacus wanted to happen. He knew this was the end for the rebels, so Spartacus added a Hollywood touch to encourage his men. He ran a sword through his horse declaring he'd either be dead soon, or they'd win and he'd have all the Roman horses he could ride. When the Roman legions charged, Spartacus went straight for Crassus in a Russell Crowe kind of way. It was time to end this thing.

He never made it. Kind of like how he never made it to Sicily, Rome, or Thrace. Story of his life. Some legionary cut down the runaway slave before he got anywhere close to Crassus. No one found his body, but you can assume it was trampled under thousands of men and then thrown into a massive grave with no marker.

To make sure the message stuck to any would-be rebels, Crassus captured six thousand survivors and crucified them along a major road to Rome. Then, one of the somebodies who had been called back, the incoming general Pompey the Great, captured the rest of the survivors and killed them. Like a bad plot line, Pompey wrote to the Senate claiming the biggest piece of victory pie against Spartacus and the uprising for himself. And everyone believed him.

intact:

Typically, when a general entered the borders of Rome, he had to dissolve his army. You know, so he wouldn't decide "dictator" sounded nice and take over the city.

The two pig heads—Crassus and Pompey—each wanted the credit, so each were set to duel. They both kept their army **intact** waiting around the gates of Rome until the Senate decided which one got to be top dog.

civil war:

See chapter two for details on the civil war and check out "The Spartacus Connection."

Finally, a deal was struck and both got to be boss. Neither was happy about the decision, but Spartacus was probably least happy of all, being dead. All this bad blood eventually led to a **civil war**, but Crassus wasn't part of it because he was dead by then, too. He'd finally gotten a foreign command like he'd always wanted and wound up

There's a reason why the emperors kept these guys on lockdown.

beheaded. Maybe justice prevailed after all, since Pompey didn't win the civil war, either. He was also beheaded in a foreign land.

After Spartacus's revolt and the civil war it helped launch, Rome switched to having emperors bossing the Senate around. With their greater power, the emperors decided they should have control of the killing machines, a.k.a. the gladiators.

First, emperors sent the gladiators out of Rome and only brought them in for special occasions. Then, the emperor started putting gladiators in imperial schools, rather than under uber-wealthy private citizens like the man Spartacus was sold to. Whenever war came close to Rome, the gladiators were kept tightly under lock and key so they couldn't start another revolt during the chaos.

In the end, Spartacus didn't stop slavery in the Roman world, and maybe he didn't care to. We'll never know for sure because neither he nor his followers wrote a word of their adventure down. He also didn't change the elites' minds regarding making people fight to the death for their entertainment— gladiator games would get bigger and bloodier in the decades to come—but he did become a symbol of hope, freedom, and equality for future generations of freedom fighters. People who believed in the right of humans to personal freedom started relating to Spartacus. He was the little guy fighting the big bully.

No one remembers Crassus or Pompey, but everyone knows the name Spartacus. Spartacus is all of us, even if we'll never know what he truly believed.

Cleopatra VII

The Famous One

The Last Queen of Egypt

Cleopatra's story is so full of fugitives, there's barely any room for ordinary people. Everyone she knew was running from someone at some point during her life. This included Cleopatra (multiple times), her entire family, both of her boyfriends, and her four kids, though not all at once. It was that sort of time in history. The first century BCE was rough. Empires rose and fell. War was as common as a cold. You could throw a scroll and hit a dozen criminals in Alexandria, Egypt's capital city. There were no cell phones.

Despite all that, Cleopatra managed to become the most powerful woman alive and the only Egyptian queen to rule without a guy by her side. Her image suffered from some ruthless press after her famous death by snake, but her life was so much more than a soap opera saga or a golden Halloween costume. Even the snake thing might not be

Cleopatra:

Was really spelled Kleopatra, which is Greek for father-loving because she was Greek, not Egyptian. We'll stick with the English-ified names throughout this chapter.

true. Instead, Cleopatra grew the Egyptian Empire to its largest extent, then ended it forever (accidentally), helped kick-start the Roman Empire (accidentally), and changed the world—all while running from her jealous enemies.

Do Not Try This at Home

Cleopatra grew up in a royal household where brother-sister relations were a little on the weird side. Not only did siblings have to play nice and share, but they also had to get married and have babies together. It sounds like a bad reality television show, but back then it was politics as usual.

Ptolemaic:

Named for Ptolemy I, the guy who started Greek rule in Egypt. See "Imitating Greatness" on page 30.

This closeness thing didn't make the royals one big happy family. Marrying one's relatives meant a lot of backstabbing and bloody endings. In the 275 years of **Ptolemaic** (pronounced tol-uh-MAY-ick) rule, only a handful of rulers died of old age. Cleopatra was not one of them.

But she was usually the smartest person in the room—when she was alive. She wrote medical papers that were legitimately good, spoke more eloquently than a politician, and knew at least eight languages, one of which was **Egyptian**, so she could communicate with the people she ruled. She was always destined for greatness—until her dad made all the common riffraff in Egypt upset.

Egyptian:

Cleopatra's ancestors were Macedonians who spoke Greek exclusively. They never bothered to learn the common language of the people they ruled in Egypt. Cleopatra was the first in her family to do so.

He kept bankrolling the powerful Romans and depleting the Egyptian treasury in the process. Those commoners started revolting, and Cleopatra bolted with her father to Rome to let tempers cool off and to ask for Roman military help to retake their kingdom. It was Cleopatra's first taste of the fugitive lifestyle.

Back in Egypt, the rebelling Alexandrians put Cleopatra's older sister Berenike in charge. Berenike definitely didn't say no to the gig, which did not make her their dad's favorite. The next year, the Romans put the sisters' dad back in charge, and he decided the only way to deal with a disobeying kid was to kill her.

When dear old dad died (of natural causes, no less), Cleopatra and her brother Ptolemy XIII were next in line for the throne. They had to get married, which was super gross considering he was ten years old and she was eighteen. Also because of the whole being related thing. Domestic bliss was not in their future.

Cleopatra pretty much ruled alone, since pip-squeak Ptolemy was more into toys than dealing with the kingdom's massive debt or stopping "allies" like Rome from being too friendly with Egyptian **stuff**. When Cleopatra started doing scary things like gaining the respect of common Egyptians, leaving her brother's name off official documents, and making decisions without him, her brother's advisors knew what they had to do—eliminate the queen.

I'm so much more fabulous than you've been led to believe.

stuff:

Like their colonies, which Rome decided would be better in Roman hands.

Like a Boss

Cleopatra had a lot of problems. From ongoing famines to a depleted treasury to sibling rivalry on a sphinx-sized scale, things were sort of falling apart

Julius Caesar:

Another one-time fugitive, but not at the time of this story.

in Egypt. Then Cleopatra made a mistake and backed a loser. Pompey the Great had helped her and her dad while they were in exile. So, when Pompey needed troops to fight against his arch-nemesis, **Julius Caesar**, in the Roman civil war, Cleopatra was quick to send supplies and soldiers to Pompey. It didn't make her popular at home.

The Egyptians had enough trouble feeding their own families thanks to all those famines, and they were really tired of all the Romans hanging around their city. Fights broke out constantly between Egyptians and Romans in Alexandria.

Cleopatra's aid to Pompey weakened her support so much that her annoying little brother managed a mutiny. It must have been impressive, since it forced Cleopatra to flee to Syria. Although she'd lost her troops, her support system, and her crown, Cleopatra decided an early retirement didn't suit her. In a matter of months, she found other troops willing to fight for her and was knocking on her brother's door once again. Even in exile, she was impossible to ignore.

That's seriously the only real picture we have of the famous queen. She wasn't supposed to look pretty—just powerful.

Back in Egypt, Ptolemy got ready to meet his sister on the battlefield when a different fugitive showed up—Pompey. Pompey had lost his battle with Caesar and had fled to his friends in Egypt with Caesar in hot pursuit. But his Egyptian friends weren't very friendly.

Ptolemy XIII had Pompey stabbed to death on his arrival and then gift wrapped his head for Caesar, hoping it might make the invading Roman leave and never come back.

Caesar was mortified by the head and not just because it was the grossest present you could imagine. It was because Pompey didn't get a good Roman death—like dying in a hailstorm of fire-tipped arrows or falling on his sword. Now that was a good Roman death. A defenseless beheading was degrading.

The Spartacus Connection

This is the civil war that Spartacus unintentionally started between Crassus and Pompey, which eventually extended to Caesar. Everyone wanted credit for taking down the mighty gladiator. Since both Crassus and Pompey got themselves beheaded, Caesar obviously won. He got to be in charge—until he wound up stabbed on the senate floor. It's amazing anyone still wanted power when it painted a blood red bull's-eye on their back.

Only manly men cry real tears.

How to make an entrance.

Cleopatra knew how to take advantage of an interesting turn of events. As of now, her brother was the legitimate ruler. If she could plead her case, however, she might win back her throne.

According to ancient sources, she met with Caesar in secret, before her brother was able to meet with Caesar, to explain why she should be put back in power. Whether she unrolled herself from a carpet, bed sheets, a linen bag, or fell from the sky in a chariot pulled by rainbow unicorns—it didn't matter. Cleopatra oozed charm, and Caesar noticed. He was mesmerized.

Because of her daring, Caesar sat the two siblings down and told them to get along or get out, which Cleopatra thought sounded perfect. At least now she had a fighting chance, instead of Caesar automatically favoring her brother. She was back in the game. Of thrones.

history-making stuff:

Including the burning of the Library of Alexandria (or at least a warehouse of the library's extra scrolls), and Caesar doggy-paddling for his life across the sea in full armor with scrolls held over his head.

Ptolemy didn't like the look of Cleopatra so cozy with Caesar, so he teamed up with their little sister, Arsïno, and attacked Caesar's army. By the end of that war, a bunch of **history-making stuff** happened, and fourteen-year-old Ptolemy lost everything, including his life.

Arsïno was captured and brought kicking and screaming to

Rome for Caesar's triumphal parade where *she* was the main attraction. This included getting marched in chains for everyone to throw rotten tomatoes at. (Although most people just felt sorry for the teenage girl.) Cleopatra didn't care too much for her traitorous little sister, but that public humiliation business looked about as fun as riding a bucking hippo. She vowed never to let anything like that happen to her.

For now, Cleopatra had it all—including Egypt and a son fathered by Caesar, whom she nicknamed Caesarion. Told you Caesar was mesmerized.

Queen of Bling

No matter how captivated Caesar was by Cleopatra, he had to return home to Rome if he wanted to stay in charge there, and Cleopatra had to marry her other little brother, who was ten, because it was tradition. No one messes with tradition.

It didn't take long for her to poison her baby brother so she could gain full control. She knew when to be cutthroat. Again, because it was tradition and she still needed to be "married" to someone in the family, she had her three-year-old son, Caesarion, become her next "husband." Obviously, that meant she pretty much ruled alone. And she did it in a truly queenly fashion.

Her court was brimming with philosophers, doctors, linguists, astronomers, geographers, and all sorts of other brilliant thinkers. Cleopatra's court was more intellectual than a rocket scientist convention. During her reign, she built monuments, finished her dad's projects, expanded Egypt's territory, and struck lucrative trade deals with neighbor kings. She was really taking the queen thing to heart and trying to improve her kingdom by helping all her people.

While queen, Cleopatra visited Rome and Caesar twice, but the last time was no family picnic. It was the Ides of March, where all the guys who were jealous of Caesar's new influence and Egyptian tendencies stabbed the dictator to death. Just to be safe, Cleopatra fled home ASAP. She was pretty used to running for her life by now.

A Woman's Touch

Julius Caesar is known for a lot of things besides his love story with Cleopatra. This guy made sure the world would never forget him. First, he made a bunch of important people in Rome nervous with all his popularity, military skills, and ambition. The Senate wanted him to come back to Rome from conquering "barbarians" in Gaul, and they wanted him to leave his army behind, which made Caesar nervous in return. Instead, he crossed the Rubicon River into Italy with all his soldiers and took control of Rome. After Cleopatra's brother killed Pompey, the way was clear for Caesar's total domination of the budding Roman Empire. Caesar turned a republic into a dictatorship and shook up Rome using a bunch of ideas he took from observing Cleopatra's rule. He used calculations from one astronomer of her court to create a new calendar and named it after himself—the Julian calendar. (Some countries still used it up until 1938!) He also planned the first public library for Rome exactly like the one he admired in Alexandria. Cleopatra's influence would continue to shape Rome for centuries to come.

Let's talk about this, guys. . . . Look, over there! A purple giraffe!

Despite Caesar's untimely death, things were finally going well for Cleopatra. Her story might not have turned into a tragedy worthy of Shakespeare if another really important Roman hadn't come calling.

Mark Antony liked wine and women, and everyone knew it— including Cleopatra. When he summoned her to provide supplies to him so he could wage war against Caesar's assassins, Cleopatra brought out the big guns to impress him: **bling** as only a queen can do.

bling:

Plays, feasts, cruises down the Nile surrounded by plush pillows, two feet of roses to wade through, and royal presents that would put Santa Claus to shame. Calling something a Cleopatran feast might not be a thing today, but for a few hundred years after her death, it meant extreme luxury as only Cleo could do.

Instead of seeing her as someone to use for money and soldiers like his own personal bank account, Antony started seeing the queen of Egypt as

This is the life.

a potentially powerful partner. Cleopatra saw the same thing in him. Soon they were an item. They did little things for each to show they cared. Cleopatra gave Antony military support, and Antony conquered land as a present for the queen. Cleopatra gave him three kids, and Antony dragged her sister Arsïno still kicking and screaming out of her exile and killed her at Cleopatra's request. Cupid at his best.

All of this fit very nicely into Cleopatra's ultimate goal of restoring Egypt back to its former size and glory. Thanks to Antony, she got new land and more taxable people to help fill Egypt's treasury. It was perfect. Unfortunately for Antony, nobody back in Rome liked all this present-giving—especially a young guy named Octavian.

Caesar's will named his nephew Octavian his heir. He didn't give Caesarion, his son with Cleopatra, anything. Octavian didn't like Antony, and he especially didn't like Cleopatra who claimed her son was Caesar's real heir.

It wasn't long before war brewed between the power couple and Octavian.

Once Antony decided to live with Cleopatra full-time in Egypt while wearing un-Roman clothes and divorcing his **Roman wife**, it seemed like he'd given up on Rome altogether. At least, that's how Octavian spun it to get Rome on his side against the foreign queen and Antony. And it worked.

Octavian got the green light to declare war on Cleopatra and Antony.

Roman wife:

Who just so happened to be Octavian's beloved sister, Octavia. In a special twist you couldn't make up, Octavia eventually raised Antony and Cleopatra's kids as her own.

Hitting Rocks on Their Way to Rock Bottom

When it came to war, Cleopatra wasn't afraid to lead her navy into battle. Sure, she got seasick the last time and couldn't engage her men, but this battle would be different. She and Antony rounded up her ships with his legions of foot soldiers and met in Greece, totally prepared to invade Italy. Octavian and his commanders also headed to Greece. There, each side stared at the other.

With stalemate holding both sides up in Greece, unpleasant things like hunger were bound to happen. Most of Antony's men deserted and joined Octavian's army, so that was pretty bad. The malaria that rampaged Antony's troops also didn't help his cause. Having a traitor leak Antony's war strategy to Octavian was the worst. At least, that's what Antony thought until his beloved Cleopatra hightailed it to the open sea during a battle, taking all her treasure and ships with her. That was the worst.

Cleopatra recognized a losing cause when she saw one, and she realized Egypt needed her more than Marc Antony. She couldn't defend her home while in Greece. So she fled back to Egypt with her ships, a fugitive from Rome now. Antony followed, leaving his men to certain death. If he was looking to rehabilitate his image, this didn't help.

Octavian pressed his advantage by setting himself up in Greece and cutting off support to Egypt from there. He wasn't giving up until the queen submitted to him. When Cleopatra realized she was at rock bottom, she tried

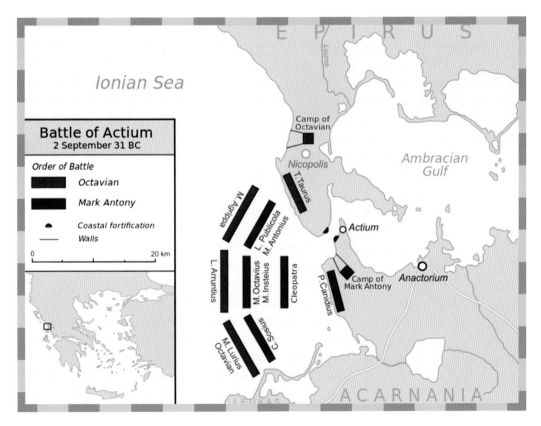

Not a good situation if you're Team Antony.

to escape to India, but that failed, too. There weren't a lot of options left, and rumor had it, Octavian wanted *her* to be the centerpiece in his triumphal parade. No, thank you. To top it all off, Antony was so depressed by this point, he was about as helpful as a swimsuit in a blizzard.

After months of back and forth negotiations between the queen and Octavian, nothing had been decided. Cleopatra wanted her kingdom left in her kids' hands—the preservation of an independent Egypt was all that mattered. Everyone else was dispensable, including both her and Antony. Octavian wanted Antony dead. Antony just wanted someone to give him a hug.

Octavian invaded Egypt, which sent Cleopatra into panic mode, obviously. Then, "someone" sent a note to Antony saying that Cleopatra had died. He was so upset that he fell on his sword in a good Roman death. Right before he died, he managed to see a very alive Cleopatra one last time before loss of blood blurred his vision. Then Cleopatra allowed a snake to bite her, or she stabbed herself with a poisoned hairpin, or she swallowed enough poison to kill a Sasquatch—sources vary. However she did it, she was dead, too.

Octavian wasn't pleased. There went his parade's centerpiece.

"someone":

Most likely Cleopatra. She probably loved him, but hard choices and duty come first as a queen. Maybe she was hoping to get a better negotiation position with Octavian if Antony was dead, but Octavian wasn't interested in negotiating.

You've Just Won Control of the Mediterranean!

Octavian had pretty much won at life, but he still had a few more loose ends to tie up. His last problem included his cousin, Caesarion, who was still alive and could possibly fight him for control of both Rome and Egypt. Caesarion tried to flee but that failed. As a gift to himself, Octavian killed Caesarion and rounded up the last of Cleopatra and Antony's kids to parade them around Rome. Then he made himself dictator like his adopted daddy, Caesar, but he didn't use the scary word "dictator." Instead, he called himself *princeps*, which sounded much nicer and just meant "first." Despite calling himself *princeps*, Octavian was really the first emperor of a new empire: the Roman Empire.

The Senate renamed him Augustus, and the new emperor went HGTV on Rome, redecorating it exactly as he wanted it. Emperor Augustus may not have wanted to admit it out loud, but Cleopatra had impressed him almost as much as she scared him. She influenced many of his new choices, including his decision to create an intellectual court atmosphere, to be considered godly, to redecorate temples with Egyptian themes, and to import obelisks and sphinxes to Rome.

The wealthy Roman elite took his cue and imported Egyptian gods, monuments, and architectural ideas like the pyramid to build fancy tombs for themselves. In order to re-create them well, they also imported Egyptian workers to build them. It was the original Egyptomania. (The next one came after Napoleon invaded Egypt in 1798 with a bunch of **savants** as well as soldiers.)

savants:

Smarty-pants thinkers and scholars who came to Egypt with Napoleon, imitating none other than Alexander the Great who also brought savants on his war travels. The savants wrote thirty-seven volumes on Egypt and brought back some keepsakes like the Rosetta Stone—the cheat sheet to deciphering hieroglyphics. It had the same message written in Greek, Demotic (the everyday language of the Egyptian people), and Egyptian hieroglyphs.

Augustus didn't want to make Rome exactly like Egypt, but he didn't mind cherry-picking from the country to create something totally new for his new empire. Something totally Roman.

In addition to all the marble buildings, conquered territory, and stability he brought to Rome, Augustus made a bunch of laws that kept women in the kitchen making him a sandwich. This kind of thinking ruled Rome and its empire, impacting future generations, and it was partly because he was awed and scared of a strong Egyptian queen.

Over the years, Cleopatra became more famous due to the hateful propaganda Augustus spewed against her. Instead of remembering her for her

I'm so special, Cupid riding a dolphin wants to touch my skirt.

courage and determination, for many, Cleopatra's name conjures images of a seductress, even though she had a grand total of two boyfriends during her entire life.

It's time that we remember Cleopatra as a cunning queen who risked everything for her country, wishing above all that it would outlast her rule. Unfortunately for her, the Ptolemys, and with them the last Greek kingdom, were finished. Egypt became a Roman province, but the proud country has never forgotten their ambitious queen.

Imitating Greatness

Ptolemy I, ancestor of Cleopatra, was a childhood friend of Alexander the Great. They were both from Macedonia, which was north of Greece, and they both went on big adventures together, like conquering the world. When Alexander died in 323 BCE, Ptolemy got Egypt as a consolation prize. Sometimes it really is all about who you know.

It wasn't long before everyone wanted to be like Alexander. Ptolemy I "redirected" Alexander's body to Alexandria, his new capital in Egypt. (He stole it.) Ptolemy wasn't exactly Egyptian royalty, so having something as special as Alexander the Great's body in town made him at least look special. Pompey asked his barber to style his hair the same way as Alexander and added "Great" to his own name. He also swiped Alex's cloak to wear. After Cleopatra's death in 30 BCE, Augustus (who also got on the floppy hairstyle train) bent over to kiss Alexander the Great's mummified body and accidentally broke off his nose.

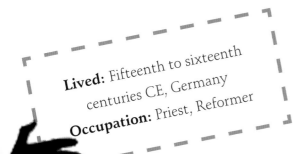

Lived: Fifteenth to sixteenth centuries CE, Germany
Occupation: Priest, Reformer

Chapter 3

Martin Luther

Medieval Social Media Guru

Extra Holy

There was nothing cushy about life in a sixteenth-century monastery. Between getting up at crazy hours each night to pray, freezing in a small cell, and being in a constant state of poverty, it wasn't the life for everyone. For Martin Luther, a **Catholic priest**, he was worried it wasn't enough—to get into heaven, that is.

> **Catholic priest:**
>
> Martin Luther was never a cloistered monk, but he liked to refer to himself as a monk, so history does, too. He was an Augustinian friar who took vows and was ordained as a priest.

It wouldn't seem that someone so intensely devoted to going to church would someday blow a saint-sized hole in the institution, but that's exactly what happened. What

Protestant Reformation:

Sixteenth-century protests against the Catholic Church that led to many Christians breaking away from the pope and his religious commands. Before the Reformation, almost all of Europe was Catholic. Lots of wars were fought and lots of people died, but the Protestants had said goodbye to the Catholic Church for good.

started out as protests in the name of reforming the Catholic Church turned into a massive split called the **Protestant Reformation**.

It's pretty impressive considering Luther managed to do it while in hiding, since the pope considered him a dangerous criminal. Funnily enough, if it were up to his father, Martin Luther would never have been religious at all. Like many parents, Hans and Margarethe Luther wanted little Martin to grow up to be a lawyer. And like many kids, Martin thought this was a terrible idea.

Smashing Dreams

Martin Luther hated school as much as the next kid. To Martin, school was worse torture than getting his brain crushed in actual medieval-style torture, but it's fair to say that most students forced to learn rhetoric, logic, and grammar would think that at least once.

Teacher's Pet Wolf

Martin Luther thought school was torture, and it certainly was worse than school today. Besides the threat of a good beating if you did something wrong or answered a question incorrectly, there was also a teacher-appointed classroom "wolf" to avoid. If a boy started speaking German instead of Latin, the wolf would report back to the teacher, who made the offender wear a donkey mask until someone else messed up. But the donkey mask wasn't enough—the kid also got a good whipping.

For a guy who hated school, Martin sure put himself through a lot of it. After spending his childhood soaking up Latin conjugations, dangling modifiers, and long-winded prose, he got a university degree and a master's degree in preparation for the lawyer life. Finally, Martin was ready for law school like his dad wanted.

Psych! Luther dropped out after two months. It wouldn't take a know-it-all to figure out that his dad would be mad. Hans had this grand plan for Martin. He wanted Martin to make lots of money so he could take care of his parents in their old age. Brilliance!

Luckily for Martin, he was too big for spankings anymore, so his parents only yelled at him when he gave up law school. But an eternity in Hell scared the bejeezus out of Martin way more than his mom's old spanking sticks.

Supposedly, Martin's change of heart happened while he was traveling home in a thunderstorm. A lightning bolt struck a little too close for comfort, and the terrified Martin cried out for St. Anne to save him. If he lived, he swore he'd become a monk.

At least, that's the story he told his dad.

Then he said something like, "Sorry, Dad, but I can't break a vow now, can I?" This didn't satisfy his father, who stayed mad at Martin for a very long time. Hans may have been the first, but he wasn't the last person to get mad at rebellious Martin and his actions.

Sounds Like a Sneeze

Martin took his vows as an Augustinian monk. Even though they were known for being an incredibly strict religious order, the Augustinians didn't give him the peace he was searching for. Instead, it made him more insecure than a shy kid at a new school. It didn't take long before Martin believed he could do nothing right. He called these insecurities and dark depressions some-

Not the Goat!

To understand Luther, you have to understand his world—sixteenth-century Europe. It was *not* like our world today. The woods to Grandma's house could be a dark, scary place with goblins and witches lurking behind every corner, waiting to sicken your best milking goat. Religion permeated every aspect of people's lives, and since most of Europe was Catholic, most everyone thought the same things. Traveling hundreds of miles in a pilgrimage was a great privilege, but dreading death, demons, and purgatory also came with the package. It was a deeply spiritual world, and one filled with danger and disease like the Black Plague that wiped out a third of the populace two centuries before. (Not to mention all the other plagues that popped up at the worst times.) No wonder Luther grew up scared to sin.

fast:

Refusing to eat for a period of time. For the religious type, fasting was an important way to deny the needs of the body to better focus on the needs of the spirit.

thing that doesn't translate well into English, but works perfect in German: *Anfechtungen.* Bless you!

If the monks said **fast** for forty days, Martin would fast for forty-one. If they said pray seven times a day, he'd pray eight. Just to make sure he had his bases covered, he'd lay in the snow for hours until another monk was forced to drag his blue butt back inside the monastery.

Martin, perpetually scared of sinning without knowing it, would make his confessor sit and listen to him for up to six hours at a time as he replayed every little detail of his life looking for any wrong-doing. Finally, his confessor couldn't take it anymore. He said Martin could turn a fart into a sin. Then, he told him not to come back until he actually did something sinful. You know, like murder.

What better way to punish the flesh?

For people obsessed with messing up, the pope gave them a safety net. He called this safety net *indulgences*, and it was sort of like credits in a spiritual bank account. A regular person sins a lot and doesn't have a huge stockpile of goodness to offset it, but a saint had good deeds coming out of their cassocks. Saints were so good, they had extra good laying around, which the pope was willing to give away—for a price, of course.

In sixteenth-century Europe, a sinner paid some earthly money to receive spiritual credit for himself or for a dearly departed family member for a sin already committed. It was like a get-out-of-jail-free card, but instead of jail, it was for **purgatory**. No surprise, the cost of an indulgence was more of the "how much you got?" variety. The rich paid more than the poor for the same credit.

purgatory:
An eternal waiting room to get into heaven.

Martin Luther wished his parents would just die already. That way, he could buy indulgences for them once and be done. The wish didn't move him to commit murder, although that would've given him something to finally confess. Instead, he jumped at the opportunity for a pilgrimage.

By going on pilgrimages and visiting relics, a sinner could also build up some good juju for the afterlife—thousands of years could be knocked off a sinner's time in purgatory simply by seeing the blood and body parts of various saints in churches and monasteries across the globe. Rome was a dragon's horde of good credit, all of it begging for sinners to come claim. It was the second holiest city to Christians after Jerusalem.

An ancient Roman skeleton all dressed up with places to go. Rome sent skeletons like these to town churches with a hefty price tag, claiming they were the remains of Christian saints.

It had everything a good Christian could hope for at the time: the thumbs of saints, a twig from Moses's burning bush, and the preserved bodies of Saint Paul and Saint Peter. It was exactly the kind of place Luther dreamed of visiting.

When he finally got to travel to Rome on Augustinian business, Luther wasn't impressed by those upstart artists in Italy like Michelangelo or Raphael, and the ancient Roman ruins reminded him of a pagan past. But the relics were a once-in-a-lifetime experience. His enthusiasm fizzled out, however, when he witnessed the holey-ness of the Holy Church.

Rome was corrupt—full of hucksters and hustlers trying to make a buck—and Luther felt duped. He returned to Germany in more personal turmoil than when he farted a lot.

Finally, his mentor came up with a plan to put them both out of their misery. He made Luther study for a doctorate. After five more years of school, Luther could teach other religious students about the Bible at the local university. A doctorate would mean a lot more work for Luther than his priestly duties. Or so his mentor hoped. If Luther was busy working, maybe he would stop worrying so much about his salvation.

The Most Epic Toilet Experience Ever

Once Martin Luther dove into teaching, he started to read the Bible even closer. That's when he noticed a lot of inconsistencies between the text and what he had been taught.

It wasn't like getting conked on the head by an apple—there was no instant flash of genius—but over the years, Luther slowly got a very different picture of Christianity than the one the priests had been peddling for centuries.

This shouldn't be surprising, since the Church maintained a pretty strict law of keeping the **Bible**

Bible:

Before the invention of the printing press by Johann Gutenberg in the 1450s, Bibles were handwritten on scrolls, they were expensive, and they were hard to obtain. Add in the fact that most Joe Schmos didn't read, and you can see why personal study didn't seem practical.

out of the hands of Joe Schmo down the street. In their opinion, it was best to leave the Bible to the experts—themselves. Next came what Martin Luther called his Tower Experience. Or should we say, his Toilet Experience.

Legend has it that Luther was on the toilet when he had his "aha" moment. Being nervous about Hell had the tendency to upset his stomach. Instead of stinking up the place for the next thirty minutes, he got to thinking—and he realized the Bible only said a person needed faith to get into Heaven. It didn't come from hiking across the Alps to see a saint's hangnail or from lying in the snow all night.

To Luther, faith alone got a person into heaven. So it really upset his delicate stomach when the Church sold indulgences as a way for a sinner to reach the Pearly Gates. Luther especially didn't like the priest who went village-to-village selling the indulgences for the pope. His name was John Tetzel.

More showman and traveling salesman than priest, Tetzel would gather a large crowd at each village he visited, sing a little ditty about getting into heaven with indulgences, and wait for the coins to roll in. However, what Tetzel didn't tell people was that the indulgence money actually went to finance the pope's party lifestyle back in Rome and to line Tetzel's own pockets.

Martin Luther didn't like a lot of things going on within the Church, but indulgences were just the worst. Tetzel rubbed him the wrong way, too, and it wasn't his singing voice.

How to Start a Revolution—By Accident

Pope Leo X: if it wasn't for him, the Reformation may never have happened. He came from a pretty rich and powerful family. You may have heard of them: the famous Medici family of the Italian Renaissance. The Medicis didn't mess around. They wanted power, so they took it. Then they used that power to get one of their own elected pope. Pope Leo X was way more interested in art than religion, though. Instead of worrying about sinning and praying like Luther, this pope worried about throwing really great parties and how pretty his apartment looked.

In order to finance all that prettiness, he encouraged indulgence selling and used the money to build up the Vatican. He hired artists like Raphael to paint murals and made his jesters ride around Rome on a white elephant named Hanno. Then, he ignored a small-time German priest named Martin Luther, thinking he was more of an ant than a giant. Oops.

Luther couldn't help asking hard questions like: if the pope had the power to bust people out of purgatory, why didn't he do it for free? Luther wrote out all his problems and posted them to the sixteenth century's equivalent of a message board—he **nailed** them to the door of his church. There were ninety-five questions or problems in total—called theses—and he wrote them in Latin.

> ### nailed:
> Or maybe he just sent them to his superiors with a strongly worded letter. Luther was good at strong words.

Only priests and academics read Latin, not commoners. Luther just wanted to start a debate with smarties like himself and hopefully get some things changed. He didn't intend to plunge a dagger straight into the heart of the thousand-year-old Catholic Church. Of course, that's not how the Catholic leaders saw it. Probably because his complaints spread like wildfire and got regular people thinking. Everyone knows nothing good comes from that.

Demons and indulgences seemed to go together to Luther.

Winning the Original Social Media Game

It all started when someone translated Luther's ninety-five theses into German, the common language. Luther didn't want that to happen—he even tried getting his original copy back—but it was way too late. Most people still couldn't read it, but the few who were literate read the pamphlet out loud for others. Then they started talking and thinking.

Uh-oh. Hearing Luther's words made others realize they weren't the only ones suspicious about that expensive **twig**.

twig:
The one that supposedly came from Moses's burning bush thousands of years ago.

After that, it took four weeks for all of Europe to know about Luther's ninety-five complaints. Luther still thought he could work within the Church to fix the problems, but the Church was done with him.

Catholic clergy fired back publicly, but they made a crucial mistake in this match. Angry clergy members still wrote their retorts in Latin. As a result, the printers couldn't give away the Catholic pamphlets, while Luther's pamphlets in German were selling like big screen televisions on Black Friday.

When Luther realized the Church was more likely to jail him than listen to him, he went on the offensive to defend his ideas. His approach was a three-pronged multimedia line of attack, and like social media today, it was a juggernaut. Music, images on woodblocks, and written pamphlets all helped get his word out about the corrupt system of indulgences, which was the sixteenth-century equivalent of hashtags and "likes." He was going viral.

The Church hounded him, demanding he take all his crazy ideas back. It wasn't good for people to be questioning the pope or the Church. One Catholic attacker got so mad, he called Luther a leper with a brain of brass, which was totally insulting. Regular people bought the pamphlets to follow the vicious back-and-forth name game like we follow Internet comments today. It was that riveting.

When the pope insisted Luther meet with clergy to be interrogated, Luther agreed, but he refused to do it in Rome, where he could expect a too-warm greeting (being burned at the stake). Instead, he stayed in Germany where he had more protection.

At the meeting, he refused to back down. There was a lot of shouting and name calling. Despite all his fancy pants schooling, Luther knew how to play dirty and swore like a sailor. He got more summons and more threats from the Catholic Church, but ignoring someone far away was pretty easy to do in sixteenth-century Europe. It wasn't like the pope could hop a plane and pay Luther a visit.

Burning a papal summons is so liberating.

Luther's old mentor freed Luther from his vows as a priest. That way, Luther could stay in hiding to write and lecture for the people who still liked what they heard. At this point, the pope really wanted to find Luther and take him back to Rome in chains, but Luther had a protector—a strong, German prince named **Frederick the Wise**.

Frederick didn't get his wise-guy nickname by being stupid. He knew the Catholic Church mostly represented Italian interests. Maybe it was time to change that. Maybe Luther, that obsessive ex-priest

Frederick the Wise (1463–1525):

Frederick was the Elector of Saxony. He did things like found a university, keep his domain out of wars, and collect more than nineteen thousand pieces of saints, martyrs, twigs, and even hay from Jesus's manger for his people to pay him money to see.

challenging the Church's authority, was the one to help. So he kept him out of the pope's reach until the pope got so mad that he threatened Luther with excommunication, which was the worst fate for a Catholic. Essentially, Luther would be kicked out of the Church if he didn't stop what he was doing and apologize to the pope and to the Church.

Instead of saying sorry with his fingers crossed behind his back, Luther burned the note from the pope publicly. In 1520 Germany, there was no better way to get his message across. The pope excommunicated him the next month.

Luther was fine with that. He'd come a long way from the scared, insecure young man he used to be. Now he was confident enough to stand up to the most powerful establishment in Europe.

A Celebrity Is Tested

Martin Luther's epic stand came at the **Diet of Worms**. Luther kept thinking this would be his last few days on earth. He was pretty sure the Church would corner him, capture him, and then torture him. He was mostly right.

First, they told Luther to quit it with the complaints; it was bad for Church business. Then, Luther needed to apologize and take everything back—or else.

Saying sorry wasn't his style, though. He stuck to his beliefs and insisted the Bible meant faith alone granted access to Heaven—not good deeds and indulgences. He added that if anyone could find words in the Bible to prove him wrong, he'd stop what he was preaching.

Diet of Worms:

This name is a little confusing. There was neither food nor worm eating involved. A "diet" was a formal meeting of non-religious leaders and Worms was the name of the town it was held in, which is a little disappointing, but things get more interesting from here.

The Church representatives couldn't find the words in the Bible to make him stop. Things didn't look good for Luther at this point.

Give me some worms! I'm starving after all this standing-up-to-the-establishment business.

If it wasn't for the quick thinking of a really smart guy, Luther probably would've been taken prisoner after his sassy speech. Yes, Frederick the Wise protected Luther once again.

First, Frederick made sure the Diet was held on German soil, and when things went sour, he hustled Luther out of town as fast as possible. He even kidnapped Luther before the Church could do it. "Highway robbers" ambushed Luther in a forest and brought him to Wartburg Castle, Frederick's stronghold.

The pope was furious. The Edict of Worms was sent out shortly after that. It was a notice telling the populace that Luther was a fugitive and an outlaw. Being an outlaw wasn't romantic—if found, anyone could kill Luther without punishment, and anyone hiding him was a criminal, too.

Frederick wasn't worried. Since "highway robbers" had been the ones to actually kidnap Luther, no one could accuse him of harboring a fugitive. All he had to do was play dumb. Safe in his hiding room at Wartburg, Luther spent the next year **translating** the Bible into German.

translating:

This was one of the first times the Bible was written in a language common people actually spoke. Now they could read and decide things for themselves, which gave them a lot of power. Scary power, according to some.

He figured everybody should be able to read the Word of God, rather than taking a priest's word for it.

Nobody minded but the priests.

Reluctant Revolutionary Turned Firebrand

Starting a continent-wide revolution isn't the easiest thing to do. Before things like smart phones, it was hard to get the word out about things. All that rhetoric and logic Luther learned in his tedious school days paid off, though, because he became quite the charmer.

He couldn't leave Saxony, since that was as far as Frederick the Wise's influence extended, but it's not like he missed Rome or anything. With the invention of the printing press in the 1450s, pamphlets didn't have to be copied by hand

Luther's desk somehow held up under the strain of his angry writing. Luther's digestive tract did not.

Goodbye, nunnery. Hello, drudgery.

one at a time anymore. They could be printed *en masse*, which means in big bunches, and sent anywhere. Luther talked and wooed people in person, while his pamphlets fresh off the press circled the continent. Technology was doing the job of reaching many people for him.

With his excommunication and the Edict of Worms, Luther was a permanent fugitive. Now he had time for other things. He filled up an acre's worth of trees writing about religion and busted nuns out of convents. He even married a former nun—a much younger, former nun who cooked and cleaned, unlike Luther. Life was way more interesting than if he'd practiced law, but Luther didn't say "I told you so" to his dad.

It Isn't Easy Being a Fugitive

Not everyone has the constitution to be a fugitive for most of their adult life. Martin Luther almost didn't, either. The strain of constantly being hounded and sought after proved to be too much—for his digestive tract. He was still obsessed with farts and was constantly having to race to the bathroom. Ulcers, heart problems, fainting, nerves, and a whole grab bag of other sicknesses upset him his whole life. Luckily, his wife turned out to be a pretty good doctor.

He certainly was no saint, not that saints were allowed in his reformed version of Christianity. During a peasant revolt founded on *his* principles, he sided with the rulers. Thousands of peasants were killed, but Luther knew the privileged rulers were more important to his cause than dirty, smelly, overworked peasants, so he backed the rich. He also didn't like how the peasants used the Bible instead of the law to voice their problems, and they disrupted the peace.

Then there was the issue of other religions. Instead of faith and tolerance, Luther took more of the "leave and never come back" approach for those who scared him—exactly the same approach the pope wanted for him. For Jews and Muslims, he wanted them expelled from Europe. If that sounds familiar, it's because Nazis in 1930s Germany quoted Martin Luther in their letters about ridding the land of Jews.

In between potty breaks, shunning Jews and Muslims, and betraying peasants, Luther found time to create a religion based on his interpretation of the Bible, pope not included. It wasn't entirely new, but there were a lot of changes, like only needing faith to avoid purgatory. This was the reformation part of the whole ordeal, and it lit the world on fire. Literally in some cases.

Religious wars were pretty much a continuous thing after Luther's complaining sparked the Protestant Reformation. His good-bye to the Catholic Church spawned more breaks all over Europe. For the pope, it was worse than a bad breakup—it was history altering. England completely abandoned Catholicism, and people like John Calvin and John Knox formed their own churches, too. It even led to the Catholics' own reformation. They called it the Counter-Reformation. Pretty catchy, huh?

Religious wars:

For more than a century, people fought over this split between Catholics and Protestants. The wars included the German Peasants' Revolt, the Dutch Revolt, the French Wars of Religion, the Thirty Years' War, the Eighty Years' War, and the English Civil Wars.

Martin Luther wasn't the first one to complain about the pope and Catholicism. Plenty of other disgruntled men like Jan Hus and **John Wycliffe** complained before him—they were just usually burned at the stake before they could change much. Clearly, the pope should have moved quicker at capturing the loud, former priest, but he didn't.

John Wycliffe:

Actually, Wycliffe died before he could be burned, so the Church dug up his body and burned it at the stake years later. Don't try to imagine the smell.

Chapter 4

Koxinga
Serious Achievement

Not to Be Confused with a Fu Manchu

Koxinga was born entitled. Being the son of one of the wealthiest pirate lords in the world will do that to anyone. That's probably why Koxinga thought he could take on the invading Manchus by himself and oust them from China. Instead of succeeding, he became a fugitive, chased from his own home. Somehow, things still turned out okay for Koxinga. While on the run, he established the first Chinese rule in present day Taiwan, igniting a five-hundred-year-old argument that still sparks today.

Koxinga actually had three names, but we'll stick to Koxinga because it's awesome and because Koxinga himself liked the sound of it. Koxinga means "serious achievement," which is a lot to live up to, especially when you consider the source. Koxinga received the title from the Ming Emperor. That's like the president of the United States naming you "Will Do Incredible Things." No pressure or anything.

Koxinga's dad, a Chinese pirate lord, also had some serious achievements to his name—which was Nicholas, by the way, a very Catholic name. In his heyday, Nicholas terrorized Ming ships. Finally, the Ming Emperor asked him to join his navy. If the emperor couldn't beat him, he figured he'd join him. The pirate lord accepted the offer and kept on terrorizing ships, but for the Mings now. It made him one of the most powerful men in China.

Everything was going swimmingly for Nicholas and Koxinga until the **Manchus** invaded.

When the Manchus arrived in the Chinese capital, Beijing, they got down to business, kicking the Mings out and launching the Qing (pronounced CH-ing) dynasty. Anybody who served the Mings could be spared persecution if they cut their hair in the Manchu style.

Manchus:

They're the guys with the red hats and tassels, not to be confused with the Fu Manchu, a mustache that looks like two wimpy noodles hanging past the chin. That's a television invention from the 1950s.

Maybe Nicholas liked the look of the Manchu queue (a long braid). Or maybe it's true: once a pirate, always a pirate. Whatever it was, Nicholas betrayed the Ming Emperor, shaved his forehead, braided the rest of his hair, and flipped sides again. To say Koxinga was horrified would be an understatement.

For Koxinga's loyalty, the Ming Emperor (who was still pretending he was emperor despite being run out of Beijing) gave Koxinga a new name: Count of Loyalty. But how did he get so loyal to the Mings in the first place?

I win. Emperors always do.

Serious Achievement

The Manchu queue: awesome fashion statement¿

In China, fathers came first. Having grown up with his Japanese mother in Japan until he was seven, Koxinga didn't see life that way. When his deadbeat dad finally remembered he existed and sent for him, Koxinga went to China and learned all about Confucianism under the Mings. He also learned how to be a pirate from his dad, but that didn't mean he had to be loyal to Nicholas. The guy forgot about him until he was seven. There was no way Koxinga would bow to the Manchus to please his dad.

When the Manchus attacked Koxinga's home, his samurai mother (who had been brought over to China, too) attacked back. She fought fiercely with the family, killing many Manchus before their numbers overwhelmed her. Instead of being taken prisoner, she plunged her own dagger into her throat. The Manchus were pretty **impressed**.

When Koxinga found out his mom had died, he took it rather poorly for a hardened soldier. He fell to the floor, sobbing and tearing his clothes apart. Then he promised lifelong revenge on the Manchus. Considering how ferocious his mother was, this wasn't good news for them.

impressed:

Legend says that the Manchus never tried to conquer Japan because of his mother's fierceness.

The Manchus thought they had one last card to play to bring Koxinga under their control. Despite the fact that Nicholas had served them China on a pirate ship platter, they took him and his new haircut prisoner. Nicholas could only gain his freedom if his son turned himself in and pledged his loyalty to the Manchus by getting his own stylish queue.

Yeah, right. To Koxinga, traitors were on their own and that included his father. Koxinga started gathering an **army**, despite only reading about how to be a general. Once the troops were assembled, Koxinga let the Manchus know exactly what he thought of them by attacking them whenever and wherever he could from both the sea and his land base on the southern coast.

He's Going All the Way

For ten years, Koxinga annoyed the Manchus in every way possible. When he wasn't gathering an army of supporters from local villages, he was raiding Manchu outposts and stealing supplies. He kept all his men and supplies on ships along the southern coast of China. That kept him mobile, but it also allowed Mazu, the patron goddess of seafarers, to protect his soldiers and his loot.

army:

Koxinga required fierceness in his men. He thought up drills called the Five Plum Flower Drill (how fierce!) and led marches and battles himself. He created a special unit called the Tiger Guard whose members had to prove their worth by carrying a five-hundred-pound stone lion around for a while.

Even though his father sent letters to Koxinga, asking him to stop and turn himself in, Koxinga wouldn't do it. Instead, he flew a banner above his ship that read: KILL YOUR FATHER, RESTORE YOUR COUNTRY! Koxinga and his dad would need more than family counseling to solve their issues.

It took a while, but Koxinga finally gathered enough men and supplies to strike at the heart of the

No one comes between me and my man!

Manchurian Qing Empire in the north: Beijing. He was going all the way.

Koxinga gathered his warships and as many as 150,000 troops and headed for the **Yangtze River**. He left one general in the south to keep an eye on his southern holdings. He probably should've left more.

Yangtze River:

It literally means "the long river" and is the longest river in Asia at 3,915 miles.

Unfortunately for Koxinga, he had a bad habit of beheading his generals if they lost a battle. Sometimes that inspired them to greatness. Other times, it left them panicky and short of breath. When the Manchus attacked the south during Koxinga's absence, his general quickly realized he couldn't win the battle. Instead of trying to fight, the general shaved his head and surrendered to the Manchus. He must have figured it was better than losing his head to Koxinga.

Things weren't going much better for Koxinga on his way to Beijing. Before he got to the Yangtze River, a huge storm struck his fleet and wiped out thousands of his men. Thousands more fled in terror, since obviously the storm meant that the sea goddess was no longer on Koxinga's side. (Really, it was typhoon season.) Paranoia reigned among the rest of the troops. Koxinga was one smooth talker, though. He held the rest of his army together and made the trek to Beijing the next year. In 1659, he finally entered the mouth of the river.

change the minds:

It also changed the mind of the Qing emperor who got so mad at Koxinga that he started chipping away at his own throne with a sword.

As Koxinga and his troops made their way north, they trounced the Manchus and picked up more soldiers along the way. They made it to Nanjing with an army of 85,000 men. That began to **change the minds** of his soldiers about their chances against the Manchus.

Happy Birthday to You

Nanjing was where Koxinga made another mistake. The city was special to him. He had studied Confucianism there as a teenager, and he didn't want

Rub a dub dub, Qings on a junk (Chinese ship).

to attack the city's residents. He wanted them to surrender peacefully. As a result, he fell for the oldest trick in the book.

The leader of the town, Viceroy Lang, told Koxinga the citizens would surrender in a month. They needed to pretend to hold out for appearances' sake so the Manchus would think they had fought bravely. Really, Lang was stalling. He knew Manchu reinforcements were on their way. In the meantime, Lang's spies infiltrated Koxinga's camps where they gathered information and set up bombs that killed hundreds of soldiers. More officers (afraid of losing their heads) fled to the Manchus and spilled their guts with whatever information they knew.

A surprise attack came on Koxinga's birthday. It was not a good present. The Manchu attack devastated Koxinga's army, forcing him to flee again and to give up his dream of marching on Beijing forever.

Instead of pausing to celebrate their victory, the Manchus decided to kick Koxinga while he was down. They destroyed his ancestral gravesites and offered money and titles to anyone in Koxinga's army who defected to the Manchu side. Koxinga could take a few defections, but the other tactic cut deep. By destroying his family's graves, his dead ancestors could no longer offer him protection and help. It was a dirty, dirty game to play in seventeenth-century China.

Dutch Formosa: Present-day Taiwan.

The Manchus also decided to cut Koxinga off from his support system. They evacuated the residents along the southern coast, torched their homes, and laid waste to the coastline. Without the villages to restock Koxinga with supplies and soldiers, he was practically alone, and his pirate reputation was in the dumps thanks to all the defeats.

But you don't get a name like Serious Achievement for nothing. Instead of seeing disaster in all this, Koxinga saw opportunity. The devastation inflicted by the Manchus left thousands of refugees. Koxinga sailed along the coast, picking up as many as he could. Then, he ferried the refugees across the Taiwan Strait to the little island known as **Dutch Formosa**. There, he set up a camp from which he could launch a new rebellion against the Manchus. The only problem now were the Dutch.

Winning the Heart of a True Momma's Boy

While women in seventeenth-century China usually stayed at home weaving and doing other "girly" jobs, not all were content with the domestic life. Like Koxinga's wives. They preferred to spend their days crafting armor and weapons, which makes sense when you think about it. How could a man with a fierce samurai mother have any other kind of wife? In fact, his principle wife, Cuiying, was said to be as tough as his mother. According to records, Koxinga and Cuiying didn't like each other at the beginning of their marriage and fought for the first ten years they were together. Then one day, as the Manchus approached their house to destroy it, Cuiying sprinted back inside and saved Koxinga's most prized possession—the wooden block that carried his dead mother's soul. Suddenly, Koxinga realized what a knockout wife he had, and from then on, he involved her in all his decisions.

The boat is leaving!

Sometimes It Pays to Be Paranoid

If someone like Koxinga takes up residence in your backyard, you can't help but worry. Rumors flew back and forth among the Dutch residents on the island. When Koxinga stopped trading with them for a few months, they thought he was blockading them. When they saw Koxinga hanging around their ports, they figured he was planning an invasion. When trade was perfectly normal, they figured Koxinga was trying to lull them into a false sense of security.

Koxinga sent letters to reassure the Dutch that all was well. He told the governor not to worry. He had sworn a death-oath to fight the Manchus. Why would he waste his time on them?

Batavia:

Present-day Indonesia where the Dutch had set up a colony.

Yet, Koxinga had learned a thing or two from the Manchus. Secretly, he began gathering his remaining soldiers for an invasion against the Dutch colonies.

The Dutch were between a rock and Koxinga. They had a rebel army hanging out in their ports, and no one seemed to care. Their governor, Frederick Coyet, insisted they needed back-up, but his bosses in **Batavia** told him to quit being a baby. Koxinga had no intentions of attacking.

Finally, negotiations between the Dutch and Koxinga began, meaning Koxinga told the Dutch what to do. He ordered them to fly their country's flag if they accepted his terms of invasion or a red banner if they preferred war.

The next morning, a blood-red banner flew from the ramparts of the fort. Coyet didn't plan on going down easy.

Koxinga's men rowed to shore where the Chinese inhabitants already living on the island met them with weapons and supplies. Things didn't look good for the Dutch. Koxinga attacked and after a short battle, won control of the open ground and sea. The Dutch stayed holed up behind their stone walls, refusing to come out and play. The long delay meant both sides fared poorly. Food reserves grew dangerously low, and malaria was doing a grim reaper act on both sides. Koxinga's mainland generals failed to keep his supplies furnished, but supplies for the Dutch had been cut off, too. Each side waited for a miracle.

Finally, after months of siege, ships appeared in the west, and they were flying the Dutch flag. The Dutch inside the sieged city cheered. Unfortunately, the ships weren't Dutch warships. They were political ships sent by Batavia to recall Governor Coyet because they thought he was too paranoid to lead Formosa anymore. When the Dutch ships spotted Koxinga's fleet and their own red banner of war at the fort, they reversed course and scurried home, hoping no one saw them.

After that, Batavia agreed that Governor Coyet had a point. Koxinga did seem intent on invading. They decided to send soldiers, but no one volunteered for the mission. Going against Koxinga seemed like a death wish. Things had finally reached a true stalemate.

Koxinga chipped away at the Dutch fort one bombardment at a time. After nine months of siege, with no hope for help from Batavia, Coyet surrendered by replacing the red flag with a white one. Once the Dutch colonists admitted defeat, Koxinga let the governor and his men quickly sail away to Batavia.

The Dutch weren't so kind to their own colonists once they arrived. They put Governor Coyet on trial for losing Formosa. He was found guilty and exiled, which seems a little excessive since they were the ones who didn't come to his aid in the first place.

We surrender. Food!

In any case, Koxinga celebrated his victory by taking down the white flag and flying his own family banner. As loyal as ever, he proclaimed this island as the eastern capital of the Mings—despite not hearing from the Ming claimant in months.

Meanwhile, the Manchus had found the last Ming claimant and disposed of him, which is a nice way of saying they strangled him. Koxinga's dream of re-establishing the Ming Dynasty was officially dead. The Manchus also killed Nicholas.

News about the Ming claimant's and his father's deaths reached Koxinga around the same time that he contracted malaria. He died of heartbreak and malaria—but mostly malaria—two months after capturing Formosa.

For two decades after his death, Koxinga's sons ruled on the island. Then the Manchus came. An old ally defeated Koxinga's heirs and talked the Manchus into bringing the island into the Qing dynasty. So. Much. Treachery.

Koxinga's Complicated Legacy

What's this all have to do with today? Well, thanks to Koxinga, Taiwan has a large population of Han Chinese descent. Yet, during the Sino-Japanese war of 1894 to 1895, Japan claimed Taiwan for themselves. Although he'd been dead for more than two hundred years, Koxinga became a central figure in their propaganda. The Japanese claimed that because Taiwan's founder was born in Japan to a Japanese mother, the country belonged to them. They—Japan and Taiwan—were destined to be together.

How to Insult Someone in Seventeenth-Century China

Being a former pirate, Koxinga liked to demand payment for protection or tribute. This worked with the villagers, but the governor of Spain's colonies in the Philippines, Manrique de Lara, was not impressed. After such a request, he wrote Koxinga a letter in which he said: "Large and small kingdoms are not made by your will alone, because your life and intellect are short and limited. You were born yesterday and you shall die tomorrow without leaving on earth even a memory of your name." Pretty harsh words, but Manrique forgot the most important part of insulting someone—making sure they hear your words. Koxinga died before the letter reached him, so he never knew Manrique's true feelings about him.

I'd rather the Mings were in charge, but I guess being divine is cool, too.

The Japanese ruled the island for fifty years until they lost it after World War II ended. Then China decided they needed Taiwan back. Once again, Koxinga's name got dragged around in an attempt to convince the locals that they belonged to China, since their founder had a Chinese father and Chinese allegiance to the Mings.

Today, the debate still rages. Taiwan is called the Republic of China, not to be confused with China itself, which is known as the People's Republic of China. Due to their similar heritage, some call for Chinese unification, while others argue for Taiwan's independence. At least everyone agrees that Koxinga was a saint for ridding the island of the Dutch. In fact, China made him an official **saint** in 1875.

Who knows what Koxinga himself would think about this debate. Loyal as always, he'd probably still try to find a way to reinstall the Ming Dynasty.

saint:
That's not to mention the Japanese, who made him a god in 1898.

Regardless, Koxinga went from being a wealthy prince to a rebel fugitive to the first Chinese ruler of Taiwan. (And that's not to mention becoming a deified saint, twice.) And he did it all before dying at age thirty-seven, which is what some would call Serious Achievement.

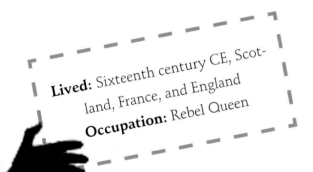

Lived: Sixteenth century CE, Scotland, France, and England
Occupation: Rebel Queen

Chapter 5

Mary, Queen of Scots

Loves a Good Conspiracy

Strategically Appealing

Mary, Queen of Scots, was a princess until she was six days old. Then she became a **queen**, but that princess persona was already embedded in her personality. She did what she wanted, and if anyone ever pointed out that she was wrong, she'd either cry or answer with an I'm-a-princess-so-what-I-say-goes. Even as an adult!

Mary rocked the glitz and glamor part of being a queen. That was the problem. From birth, she was adorable, and every king in Europe wanted her for his daughter-in-law. Henry VIII of England went so far as to invade Scotland twice to force the toddler into marriage with his son. His Rough Wooing tactics turned into an eight-year war, but no *I do's*.

queen:

Mary was the first queen regnant of Scotland, which meant she was a queen by birth, not because she married a king.

To escape King Henry's unwanted advances, Mary's mom hid the toddler in a secret chamber, then snuck her out of the castle at the first opportunity. It was Mary's first time on the run, but it wouldn't be her last. After that, it was five long years of playing musical castles to dodge the uninvited English suitors before Mary ultimately fled to a foreign country. This is the story of Mary's unhappy life—the only queen to ever sit on the Scottish throne.

No One Likes a Stalker

King Henry VIII wanted Scotland's tiny queen as his son's wife so badly that he accidentally pushed her right into the arms of his archrival, France. Henry's strategy for getting what he wanted included slashing and burning Scottish villages to the ground to scare people into accepting his

I can't help how cute I am.

wishes. Obviously, the Scots weren't impressed, and they asked the French to help get the queen as far away from Henry as possible.

French help came wrapped in another marriage proposal. Mary could live in France, learning how to pronounce *heureuse* properly (which means happy) but only if she married the crown prince, the future King Francis II. The Scots were much more comfortable with funny sounding words than they were with Henry, so they agreed.

For thirteen years, Mary pirouetted, wrote poetry, ate goose livers, and fell in love with France. She charmed everyone, except her future **mother-in-law**, who was not charmed at all. Mary also grew up a very good Catholic, unlike Henry VIII's kids who were Protestant. What Mary didn't grow up being was Scottish, despite being Scotland's queen.

mother-in-law:
The formidable Catherine de Medici who ruled France with an iron fist.

When the time came for Mary to fulfill her end of the bargain, the twelve-year-old queen said yes to the dress. She married Francis with more pomp than a Parisian poodle at Notre Dame, and she did it in a white dress. While a common wedding choice today, white was usually saved for funerals in France, but Mary knew it complemented her skin perfectly. She wasn't one for tradition, although some might call her defiance an omen. A bad one.

Mary's father-in-law died a year after the wedding, and she became **queen consort** of France, in addition to being queen regnant of Scotland. So far, so good. Mary had everything she needed, including a huge wardrobe and enough jewels to put a diamond mine to shame.

queen consort:
The wife of a reigning king.

But Mary's story was more tragedy than fairy tale, and the good life only lasted for another year. Soon, she was in her favorite color all the time—white—but this time for mourning. Her mother died, then her sickly, stammering husband died before they could seal the deal with any kids. Catherine de Medici made it pretty clear she didn't want two widow queens hanging around the palace, especially one that was childless and, therefore, worthless. All Mary could contribute to France now was her witty conversation, which Catherine didn't care for anyway.

The best place for Mary was back in Scotland. Henry VIII and his son were both dead, and Elizabeth, another queen regnant, was in charge of England, so Mary wouldn't have to worry about marriage proposals from the English.

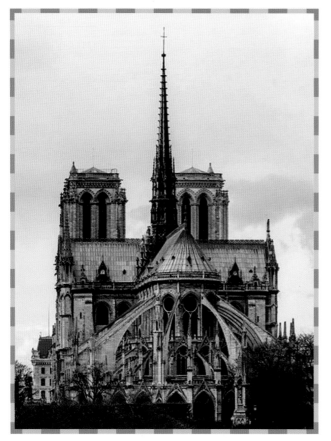

Notre Dame—a wedding venue fit for a double queen.

Unfortunately, the Scottish people didn't really want their queen anymore. While Mary danced her nights away in France, the people of Scotland had decided to change religious allegiance from Mary's Catholic faith to the newfangled Protestant faith. That switch meant a Catholic queen wasn't welcome. So Mary went from being irresistible to dispensable. Not accustomed to being ignored by anyone, Mary planned to jump right into governing her country, despite never being educated to rule a whole country alone. Anyone could see this was a recipe for disaster.

Bad Feelings Are Usually Right

Mary had a lot of things going against her when she returned to Scotland for her throne. Her management skills were subpar, she was Catholic in a chaotic Protestant atmosphere, and she identified as French rather than Scottish. To make matters worse, she was a girl when everyone knew boys should be in charge. Despite all that, she got off to a good start in her birth country.

She didn't want to start a civil war in Scotland between Protestants and Catholics like her mother-in-law, Catherine de Medici, let happen in France, so Queen Mary immediately agreed to allow everyone to do their own religious thing. She was the first ruler to show religious tolerance in England or

Scotland. She called for important meetings about religion and actually went to them. Sure, she brought her embroidery with her, but that was so no one would kick her out. Her council members all figured her **dainty** girl body couldn't do two things at once, like sew and listen.

It wasn't until she caught sight of a pretty boy that her life of wrong choices began in earnest. She always was a sucker for pretty things.

Henry Stuart, a.k.a. Lord Darnley, was tall, not dark, but still handsome, and he made Mary swoon. Even better than good looks, Henry Stuart had **Tudor** connections, just like Mary. Which was perfect since Mary thought she should be England's queen, too. Extra Tudor blood would strengthen her claim to the English throne. Darnley had some downsides, though. He was nineteen, immature, and had more loose screws than a hardware store, but Mary still wanted to tie the knot.

dainty:

And by dainty, start picturing a woman almost six feet tall, when the average man was a head shorter. Maybe it was all those goose livers?

Tudor:

The Tudor dynasty in England began with Henry VII, who had a lot of kids. Mary and Darnley were both descended from his daughter, Margaret Tudor, while Elizabeth I was descended from his son, Henry VIII.

Errs of an Heir

Mary liked to remind people, especially the English, how closely related to Elizabeth she was. Obviously, she should be Elizabeth's heir. While not exactly true, since there were other Tudors floating around England, Mary was an obvious choice—except for the whole Catholic thing. England was pretty gung-ho in their pope-hating, and Mary wasn't. Secretly, Mary thought she was way more legit than Elizabeth. They both descended from Tudor blood, but Elizabeth's mother's marriage to Henry VIII wasn't recognized as legal by the pope, and Mary hung on every word that came out of the pope's mouth. As a result, Mary believed she was the rightful queen of England, and she had a point. Just not the governing know-how.

Elizabeth didn't like to be reminded of this fact. Instead, she drew up a treaty asking Mary to renounce her claim to the English crown. Mary kept putting it off, and then she died.

Hard to tell, but the left puffed-up poodle is Darnley and the right one is Mary.

Part of the reason for Darnley's bad behavior was his parents. They told him how great he was even though he hadn't done anything great. The next reason was his wounded pride. Mary didn't trust him enough to make him king of Scotland. Instead, he simply became the queen's husband (called a king consort), which, despite all the jewels, good food, and parties, still meant he wasn't the boss. Then, Mary became pregnant, and it wasn't the prospect of poopy diapers bumming Darnley out. He knew he'd be bumped further down in importance if the baby was a boy, since his son would become the next king, not him. Lastly, Mary liked to listen to David Riccio, an Italian singer, until late at night, and that made Darnley pretty darn jealous. When Mary promoted Riccio to her personal secretary, Darnley let a bunch of his hotheaded noble friends talk him into the world's stupidest plan. Murder.

Darnley was the opposite of brave, but he had a violent streak. While the queen entertained guests at a private dinner, Lord Darnley & Co. burst into the room, waved their daggers like avengers, dragged a cowering Riccio from behind Mary's full-bodied gown, and left him dead as a dodo. Mary was six-months pregnant at the time, and the murder left her shocked and terrified for her own life. She managed to keep it together long enough to escape the castle and flee to safety until her baby was born.

It was a boy.

Time to Hire Better Advisors

Now that she finally saw the real Darnley, Queen Mary wanted a divorce. She knew, however, that a divorce would prevent James, her newborn son, from being the legitimate heir to the throne in some people's eyes. So a few of her nobles took matters into their own hands. They told her they'd find a way to get rid of the king consort. *Wink, wink.*

Less than a year after Riccio's murder, an explosion rocked the queen awake. Someone had tried to blow up one of her castles. It was far from sub-

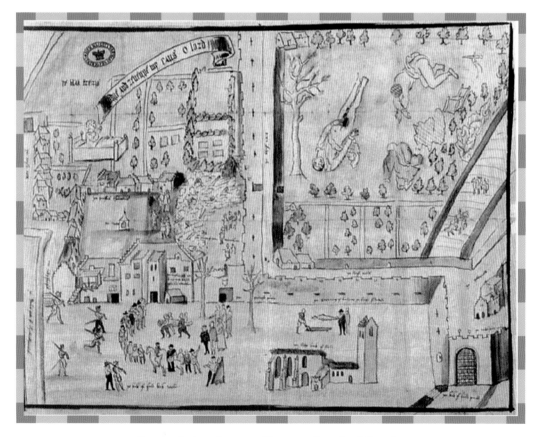

One explosion plus one pillow equals a dead Darnley.

tle, but the guy who planned it was about as subtle as a naked, screaming soccer fan. When they found Darnley's body in the gardens outside the castle, it was clear that the explosion hadn't killed him—suffocation by strangulation had. The explosion was simply a cover-up for murder.

Having two dead husbands didn't exactly make for a great track record for the Queen of Scots, but Mary was about to take bad decision making to a new low. Lord Bothwell, the not-so-subtle gunpowder fanatic, kidnapped Mary and pressured her into marrying him three months after Darnley's death. Since Mary didn't have much in the way of a support system to help her escape, she agreed. Her decision scandalized pretty much everyone, including her cousin, Elizabeth I of England. Mary and Elizabeth used to write weekly to each other. Now their letters were catty excuses for diplomacy.

The marriage controversy lit the fuse of an already explosive Scotland. Unhappy Scottish nobles marched to battle against Mary and Bothwell while keeping baby James locked up far away from his mother. (They also converted James into a good Protestant boy.) When Bothwell offered to do single combat to settle the conflict, it seemed he might have kingly guts after all. When his offer was accepted, he realized something important—that he might actually have to fight.

That didn't sound fun to Bothwell, who snuck away and left Mary to surrender. Her unhappy nobles locked her up in a dreary little fortress in the

At least there were no Loch monsters in this lake. Mary had enough problems.

middle of a lake and threw away the key. Then, they forced Mary to **abdicate** in favor of her toddler-sized son or to find herself in that lake— and not for a nice swim.

abdicate:
To give up one's throne.

At this point, most people would throw in the towel. Life as a queen hadn't worked out, and there had been more bad plots and diva personalities than daytime television. But not Mary. She put her legendary charm to good use for the next year in order to talk one of her jailers into helping her escape from her island prison. One dark night, her jailer helped Mary dress up like a servant, commandeer a boat, and, once they got to shore, wrangle horses to ride for a supporter's castle. There, Mary gathered another army to end Scotland's civil war. That would have been great, if she'd won (she didn't).

In another spectacularly miscalculated decision, Mary didn't try to rally her troops, and she didn't surrender. She did what she knew best. She fled in disguise, but to the worst place in the world for her—Protestant England.

Mary still hadn't given up her idea of being the queen of England as well as Scotland, and she had been dragging her bejeweled feet when it came to signing a treaty with Elizabeth that would end Mary's right to the English throne. Despite annoying the reigning monarch with her long-standing refusal, Mary still thought England was safer than Scotland. This was her worst decision yet, but not her last.

Sister Queens and Sister (Um, Cousin) Rivalry

Unlike Mary, Elizabeth I already knew how hazardous to her health being on the throne was. She had seen woman after woman thrown away by her father, Henry VIII, and had been thrown away herself at one point. Being queen was serious business. Mary, having always lived in a golden cage, didn't know anything about serious business unless it was looking seriously perfect for every occasion.

Elizabeth didn't want this perfect princess around. She had a lot going on as a lone woman ruling a Protestant country surrounded by rabid Catholic monarchs in France and Spain. Letting her cousin whip the people into rebellion qualified as a no-brainer bad idea. Anyway, now that Mary was off the

Mary's escape: The old bait-and-switch works every time.

Scottish throne, her son (who was Protestant thanks to those nobles) would keep Scotland out of England's affairs. It didn't make sense to put Mary back in charge in her home country.

Mary had a different perspective. She figured it'd be a short stay in England before Elizabeth helped force her treacherous nobles to give her back her Scottish throne and her brainwashed son, and to ink her in as the heir to England. Win, win, win. Elizabeth figured the only way Mary was leaving England was in a **casket**. Technically Elizabeth had no legal grounds for keeping Mary prisoner in England, but she wasn't sure what to do with her fugitive cousin.

casket:

At first, Elizabeth was horrified for Mary's sake—nobles should *not* treat their queen like that— but soon, Mary became a big ulcer on Elizabeth's leg that refused to go away.

In theory, Mary was the best option for Elizabeth's heir and the Queen of England needed an heir. But she didn't trust Mary's ruling ability. Mary had made some pretty awful choices so far, and Elizabeth didn't want England to fall through her flighty fingers. And that was without knowing what terrible choices Mary would make in the future—like trying to become Queen of England with or without Elizabeth.

Taking the throne of England might have stayed in Mary's dreams if some of Elizabeth's Catholic nobles hadn't warmed to the thought of a Catholic ruler. Especially a pretty Catholic. Even the pope thought this was a great idea, and he did his part by **excommunicating** Elizabeth.

excommunicating:
The pope kicked her out of the Catholic Church, which probably made Elizabeth laugh since she was Protestant.

Even though Elizabeth had put Mary up in stylish digs, had given Mary servants, and had let her cousin embroider to her heart's content, which seemed like a much better life than the constant running Mary was used to, Mary continued to find herself at the center of conspiracies. Ones that usually involved foreign invasions, a dead Elizabeth, and herself on the throne of England and Scotland.

The first plot was mostly talk, but it involved the Spanish invading England to place Mary on the English throne. Elizabeth's spymaster quickly put all the conspirators minus Mary on the rack, then sent them to the axe-man. After that failure, he doubled Mary's prison guard so she wouldn't try to flee to Spain.

For twelve years, Mary kept her head down in regard to plots, but not in her desire to be queen of England and Scotland. She sent letters to anyone who would listen about

Mirror, Mirror on the Wall

For years, Mary asked her cousin for a face-to-face meeting. It never happened. By the end, Mary was convinced that if Elizabeth could see the whites of her eyes, Elizabeth would love her and make her the next queen of England. Elizabeth, however, didn't want all that charm and beauty oozing around her. Vanity had something to do with it. Elizabeth had caught smallpox in 1552, and while what didn't kill her did make her stronger, it also gave her a pockmarked face. So she always found a way out of that personal meeting. Mary moaned about it all the way to the scaffold.

The code Mary used to secretly communicate with her co-conspirators was actually being read by Elizabeth's spymaster.

how unhappy she was as a prisoner. When the next opportunity fell into her lap, Mary couldn't help but take it. Again, it involved a foreign invasion by Spain to get Mary on the English throne, and again, the conspirators were caught, sent to the rack, and this time, hanged.

Queen Elizabeth got the message. Mary wasn't good at being in-waiting, and the Spanish ambassador clearly had to go. Elizabeth confined Mary to a castle and enacted a new law that made it illegal and punishable by death to plot against the queen—namely, herself.

Mary must have thought Elizabeth wasn't serious, because two years later Mary was at it again. Part of it wasn't her fault. Elizabeth's spymaster wanted to catch Mary in a trap, so he appealed to the schemer in her. He sent her secret coded letters about her favorite pastime—plotting to become queen of England with the help of a Spanish invasion. Supposedly, Mary didn't say no to the proposal. The trap was sprung.

Feeling excited about her future, Mary went out for a horseback ride. She expected freedom and the throne any second, and when she saw a bunch of men riding towards her, she figured today was the day. It wasn't the great rescue she was expecting. Instead of being whisked to the throne, like in a fairy tale, she was whisked to a courtroom and her rooms were searched. She pled not guilty, but it didn't matter. Elizabeth had finally decided the Queen of Scots had to go, and not back to Scotland.

An alive Mary caused way too much trouble, and it was making all of Europe antsy. Spain might really invade and take control of England, all because Mary couldn't accept the facts. Nobody wanted her.

How to Fail at Life

Despite all the plots against her, Elizabeth still hemmed and hawed about killing her cousin. They were both anointed queens—was nothing sacred? Elizabeth's nobles wouldn't do for her what the Scottish nobles had once done for Mary. There was no *We'll take care of the problem. Wink, wink*. Even though Elizabeth hinted a few times that it might be better if Mary suddenly dropped dead.

On February 1, the nobles finally got Elizabeth's signature on a death warrant after months of dallying and fake-outs, and they whipped that important sucker away before Elizabeth could change her mind, again.

After nineteen years of English imprisonment, Mary was rushed to the executioner's block on February 8, 1587. The executioner needed two tries to get her head off. All of England celebrated Mary's death with bonfires and banquets, except for Elizabeth who ranted that her ministers had done it all so fast and without keeping her properly informed. Did she really not want her cousin killed, or was it all for show? Nobody knows.

After spending most of her life on the run, Mary, Queen of Scots continued to change history after her death. She had failed at the fugitive thing, and instead of taking over Scotland and England, she caused controversy, plots, and wars wherever she went.

invaded:

The Spanish also didn't appreciate Elizabeth stealing all their gold on the high seas.

Spain finally **invaded** England, in part to avenge Mary's death and to put a real Catholic queen on the throne once and for all. Although Spain had the greatest fleet of ships in the world—the Spanish Armada—Elizabeth defeated them. Now England was on its way to becoming the most powerful empire in the world, and England never went back to Catholicism.

James:

The same James who tangles with the Pilgrims in chapter six.

Elizabeth finally chose a man. She would never wed, but she still needed an heir. Mary's son, **James**, was the perfect fit. He had Tudor blood, a royal upbringing, and the Protestant faith, just like Elizabeth. On Elizabeth's death, James became king of Scotland and England, uniting the two countries for the first time under his Protestant name, Stuart.

It also meant that every British monarch since that time has been a descendent of Mary, not Elizabeth. In the end, Mary got what she wanted. Sort of.

Long Live the Queen

Scotland and England are still united today. In September 2014, Scots were given the opportunity to vote for their independence from England. Fifty-five percent voted "Nae," which was enough to keep the two countries together as part of the United Kingdom, for now.

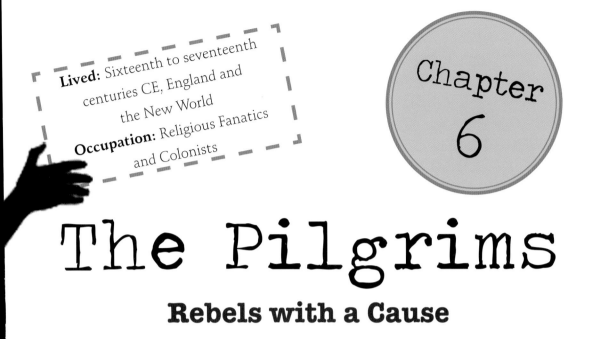

Lived: Sixteenth to seventeenth centuries CE, England and the New World
Occupation: Religious Fanatics and Colonists

Chapter

6

The Pilgrims

Rebels with a Cause

It's Not All Turkeys and Treason

Once upon a time, people searching for religious freedom decided to leave an oppressive society and settle in a fantastic new land of promise. It was totally empty except for a few nice natives and tons of wild turkeys. These pilgrims finally had the ability to worship how they wanted, but not the skills to farm well. It was winter, and these newcomers were starving. Luckily for them, one of those nice natives named Squanto gave the people some corn and taught them how to properly plant it in order to survive their next winter. Everyone celebrated the harvest with three days of feasting.

It's a familiar story, but is any of it true?

It's certainly true that the Pilgrims get a lot of great press as the forefathers of America, and they definitely knew how to eat. We celebrate their celebration with a feast of our own—Thanksgiving. They also embraced the fugitive lifestyle, searching for religious freedom in any place that would take them. All the other stuff like buckles and turkeys . . . well, read on and try not to be too disappointed.

Yeah, no. Not much is true here, not even the buckles.

Girlfriend Problems

It all started in 1534, when King Henry VIII wanted to get divorced from his wife in order to marry his girlfriend. He had to ask permission from the pope, which was tricky. The pope was the head of the Catholic Church in Rome, and he didn't think divorce was the best idea Henry ever had. So he said no and denied Henry the **true love** of his life—Anne Boleyn.

Henry wasn't a king for nothing, though. He got out his big, red, editing marker, changed the official religion in England from Catholicism to Henry-ism (although he called it the Church of England), and made everyone switch with him. Some people loved it. Others hated it. The ones who hated it tended to be Catholic and they tended to end up dead.

true love:

Which lasted until Henry beheaded Anne and married four more women. "The course of true love never did run smooth." (That's a little Shakespeare for you.)

All Those Ps!

Protestants: *Starting with Martin Luther in Germany, Protestants protested the Catholic Church's ideas and formed their own church.*

Puritans: *Protestants who wanted to purify Henry's Church of England.*

Separatists: *Puritans who decided purifying wasn't enough and wanted to split off to form their own church (sure, Separatists doesn't start with a P but they are important, anyway).*

Pilgrims with a big P: *Separatists who put their money where their mouth was and actually left England to build their perfect community.*

Pilgrims with a little p: *The people who travel to holy sites (such as churches and shrines) and holy lands (such as Jerusalem and Rome) for various reasons are called pilgrims on a pilgrimage.*

The people we call **Puritans** were okay with the divorce thing, and they loved the new religion thing since it was closer to the Protestantism over on the continent (see chapter 3). The Puritans just didn't think Henry put enough thought into his new church. To be fair, he really hadn't changed much besides putting himself in charge. There was still a lot of kneeling, fancy hats, wedding rings, and other Catholic-y stuff. The Puritans wanted to purify the church even more.

Puritans:
A nickname given by Catholics to the group of Protestants who wanted to purify the Church of England further. It wasn't supposed to be a nice nickname. The Puritans preferred to call themselves "Saints."

Then there were the Separatists—such as our future Pilgrims—who wanted to break away from the church entirely because the new church needed more than a facelift. To them, it needed a new face. Henry's church was beyond reforming.

By the time King James I took the throne in 1603, England was a little jumpy. A Catholic man had recently tried to blow up the government; Catholic Spain kept threatening to invade the country; and crazy people kept bringing King James new ideas for the church they wanted him to change, like having congregations be in charge of religious matters, not the king. Treason and treachery!

King James didn't appreciate being told by riffraff that he was doing things wrong, and he shot down almost all of the Puritans' suggestions for change. Although it was a Catholic fanatic who tried to blow him up with a gunpowder plot, who knew what the Separatist fanatics were capable of? So when somebody didn't go to the right church at the right time while saying the right words, that person found himself on the authorities' Most Wanted list. To the king, it was worse than treason to not accept his church.

S.S.:
Sower of Sedition—in other words, a rabble rouser.

Unlike the rulers before him, hanging wasn't James's go-to method of diplomacy, but he still used it occasionally. Separatists could also be thrown in prison, tortured, have **S.S.** branded on their foreheads, be fined, or forced into poverty. The Separatists decided to hightail it out of England before any of that happened. Nooses aren't the prettiest necklaces, and no one fancied the rack.

One tiny problem remained—leaving England without permission was illegal. But laws never stopped them before.

I'm the king, and I'm pretty sure the king is in charge!

Stealth Was Not Their Middle Name

The leaders of these rabble rousers figured Holland would be the perfect place to go underground. Maybe they chose Holland because it had awesome scenery thanks to all those rolling hills and windmills, or maybe they chose it because of all the genius potential there. (Baby Rembrandt, future famous painter, was crawling through

My necklace has splinters.

tulip fields in Leiden at this point in history.) But, more importantly, they knew Holland didn't get too worked up over religious issues.

The Separatists tried to get their flock over to Holland, but failed. A hundred people booking passage on a boat looked a little suspicious, but that didn't actually tip off the authorities. The ship's captain did.

Authorities swooped in and took away every one of the Separatists' books and money. Then they put the fugitives in time-out (a jail cell) to let them think about what they did. After a month, King James released them, except they had nowhere to go back to. They'd gambled the house and lost big. Seriously. They had no houses and no money. And it was winter.

The Separatists tried to flee the country again a few months later. This time, they hired a more reliable captain, but their problems weren't over. The authorities were still on to those sketchy Separatists and watched their every movement. When a bunch of people tried to leave the country again, the authorities arrested anyone they could catch. Which was all the slow moving women and children.

That looked bad. Arresting a bunch of women and their crying kids because they couldn't run fast enough didn't make the best impression on the rest of the citizens. Especially since, in those days, everyone knew the women were just following their husbands. The authorities were forced to let all the Separatists go, including the few men who volunteered to stay with the women. It was either that or let them become **martyrs** in jail.

martyrs:
People who suffer and are usually killed for their beliefs. If a bunch of women and children were rotting away in jail, the citizens would feel sympathy for them, which didn't look good for the authorities.

It took a few more months of secret crossings, but eventually the Separatists got the gang back together in Amsterdam. Everything was sort of great. They lived in a city now, instead of in villages, which wasn't exactly sunshine and rainbows but at least they were free.

It took less than a year of big city living before the religious group moved on to greener tulip fields—Leiden, Holland. It still wasn't the home they had left behind, but for more than a decade they could worship how they wanted—which was a lot—and do what they wanted. This included printing up all kinds of snarky newspapers to smuggle back to England about stupid King James. One day, the Separatists believed, everyone would see their way was the best way.

Except people didn't. James asked the Dutch to hand over the unruly Separatists on the double, and when that didn't work, he sent in his own agents to find them. Loudmouthed Separatist printers like William Brewster had to go into deeper hiding to avoid the rack. The one poor sucker the English authorities managed to find died in prison. (Brewster wasn't found until he turned up with the rest of the Pilgrims in Plymouth.)

Also, the Dutch were really, well, Dutch. It's hard being a foreigner in a new country, and the Dutch didn't help. They never fully let the English into their society, and they were into strange things like painting for fun,

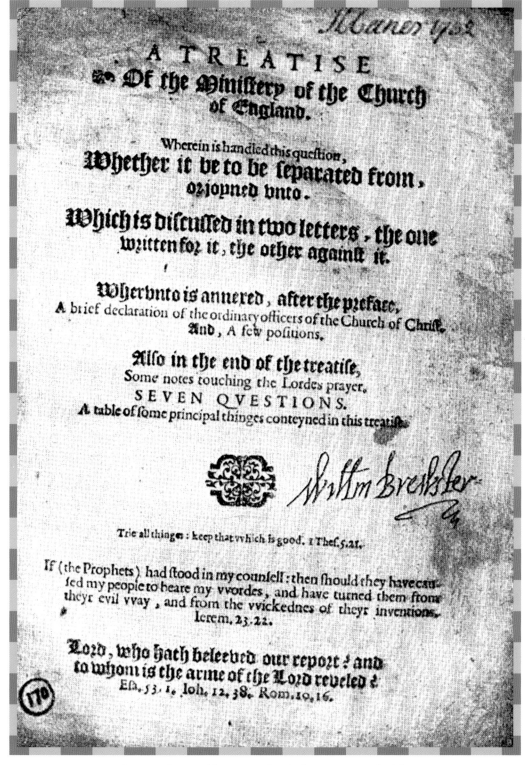

Brewster's pamphlets: enough to lock away a guy for life.

dancing, listening to music, and having disposable income. Good times for the Separatists included reading the Bible and giving their extra money to their congregation. This was more disturbing than picturing King James in his underwear. Even worse, the fugitives' kids were growing up as Dutch as the wooden clogs on their feet.

There were also rumors circulating that the Spanish were going to invade Holland. King James I might make life miserable for the Separatists, but the Spanish king was Catholic. He would end their miserable lives. Eventually, the leaders of the colony decided it was time to shake things up. They couldn't go back to England, and they couldn't stay in Holland, so maybe it was time to think outside the reliquary box and sail into the unknown. Preferably somewhere warm—like South America! Who wouldn't want to live in "perpetuall spring" as **William Bradford** called it?

William Bradford:

A Pilgrim himself, Bradford was the unofficial biographer of the Pilgrims, and he sailed with them from Holland on the *Mayflower*. Six months after landing, he became their governor in the New World.

This story might have turned out quite differently if the Pilgrims hadn't decided tropical climates were dangerous, what with exotic diseases and all. Instead, they'd go to where the English had already gone before—the New World (the future United States of America, of course).

Not Bitter, Just on to Bigger and Better Things

The Pilgrims weren't the first Englishmen and women to come to the New World. The whole Captain John Smith and Pocahontas saga had already happened a few years ago at the Jamestown colony. In fact, Pocahontas had also already sailed to England, met King James I, and died of disease by the time the Pilgrims were itching to set their non-buckled boots on Virginian soil.

There were already English laws governing this new land, too. Not just anyone could set up shop and start their own colony there—not even fugitives. Before they could go, the Pilgrims had to have the go-ahead and a game plan. Otherwise King James would send his agents to the New World and slap them all in chains. The Pilgrims also needed money, which was a problem. They didn't have any.

After working low-end jobs for years in Leiden, gold was in short supply, and it takes a lot to start a new society. They needed money to buy essential supplies like food and clothes, and they needed a boat and a crew who knew how to sail it. So the Pilgrims sent two of their men back into the lion's den—London. Their goals included finding money and getting permission to settle in the New World. They turned to investors for money and the Virginia Company for land—the same company from the Pocahontas saga.

Investors and the Virginia Company were willing to risk money up front in hopes of making a bunch more once the colonists got settled. The Virginia Company had another reason for taking a risk on the Pilgrims: redemption.

Over the years, the Virginia Company had gotten some bad press. Their Jamestown colony killed more people through disease and starvation than it kept alive, and it was getting harder to talk regular folks into risking their necks by going there. Pretty soon, King James was going to have to start sending convicts to Jamestown in order to spruce up his namesake. The English *needed* another working colony and fast.

By this time, King James didn't care if the religious group left forever, as long as they didn't bother him anymore. He said the Separatists could leave the Church of England and settle the New World as long as "they carried themselves peaceably." He never clearly said they could practice whatever religion they wanted, but the Pilgrims knew he was cool with it.

The investors were happy, too. All they cared about were cute, little beaver butts. Europe was beaver-hat crazy, and since they'd killed their own native beaver population for their addiction, the New World was a hotspot for beaver pelts. Investors didn't want to risk their own lives, but they'd risk a bit of money. The Pilgrims would need to fish, trap, trade, and haul lumber to make a profit for their investors. According to the deal, they had seven years to make it work.

The Virginia Company gave the Pilgrims permission to settle in Virginia, and the investors helped them raise money to buy things like ships and food.

The boat couldn't hold all of the Leiden congregation, however, so who got the disease-and-disaster-ridden ticket?

William Brewster was definitely going because King James still wanted to capture him. One hundred and one other passengers joined him, but they weren't all Pilgrims with a capitol P. Some were regular John and Jane Does who also wanted a fresh start or a new way to make a living. The Pilgrims called those people "Strangers." These hooligans were fishers, merchants, and dreamers. Religion didn't matter much to them, but like the Pilgrims, they were looking for new beginnings. Finally, the Pilgrims had all the kinks figured out.

Only one problem. By the time the Pilgrims set sail, planting season was way over. They should have been harvesting their crops for the coming win-

I miss windmills.

ter, not puking their brains out during sea storms in the Atlantic. This was going to bite them in the butt once they reached the future North American shores sixty-six days later.

All those sea storms blew the *Mayflower* practically to the moon. According to their deal with the Virginia Company, the Pilgrims were supposed to land in Virginia and build their colony there. They wound up in Massachusetts. The crew knew a mistake when they saw it, but instead of risking more time sailing, they dropped anchor in modern-day Cape Cod and called it good enough. Areas of Cape Cod had already been **cleared** of trees and Native Americans due to previous Europeans and their **plagues**, so it was a pretty ideal spot to set up camp.

Since the Pilgrims had decided not to continue on to Virginia, *some* people considered themselves under no laws. (The Strangers, of course.) Everyone was getting a little edgy. Someone had to step up and take charge before things got violent. Luckily, William Brewster, who had escaped King James and had a college education, was ready for the job.

Brewster probably wrote up the Mayflower Compact for the men in the group to sign. The Mayflower Compact was a bunch of ideas on how to live peaceably together. Mainly, the Compact stated that James is great and all, but that the Pilgrims were going to pass their own

cleared:

It's much easier to build a town if you're not starting from scratch. The Pilgrims staked out Plymouth on Cape Cod after finding plowed fields and houses from when a local Native American tribe called the Patuxet lived there. The Patuxet living in that particular village had been decimated by a plague, which really doesn't do justice to how many died. All of them.

plagues:

It's speculated that the arrival of European diseases is the single greatest event in American history. Ninety percent of the native population died from disease, paving the way for European domination over all this "empty" land. Compare that to the Black Plague of fourteenth-century Europe, which only offed about 30 percent of the population. The Native Americans were facing an apocalypse of dinosaur proportions.

You're welcome.

laws if need be. And they were going to be "just and equal." James obviously should have seen this coming.

Considering they arrived only six weeks before the start of winter and no one brought enough food, livestock, or know-how to make it through the tough season, the Pilgrims were lucky to survive at all. Instead, only about half of the colony died, and no one resorted to cannibalism, unlike at Jamestown. Score!

When Squanto found the colonists in the spring, they were half starved and half dead. Squanto was a sympathetic Patuxet Native American who spoke English thanks to being sold into slavery in Spain. He'd escaped Spain (another fugitive!), traveled to England, and hopped a boat home where he found his village decimated from plague. Apparently he didn't hold grudges, because he later taught the colonists how to survive. He showed them how to plant native foods for the next winter, how to fish, and how to find beaver butts so they could pay their debts and not have to eat the sickly kids.

Sachem Massasoit, a Wampanoag leader, formed an alliance with the Pilgrims after a plague wiped out most of his people. He thought it would be beneficial to team up with the men with guns in order to fight his enemies, and Squanto, now living with Massasoit, helped broker the deal. The Pilgrims got help from all around, which should make any-one very thankful.

Sachem:
Leader.

The next harvest season in 1621, the Pilgrims decided to feast. When Massasoit and the Wampa-noag gathered to feast with them, they brought ninety people and five deer. Harvest festivals were familiar to both cultures. There was no football, but there were games with balls and feet. Turkey may or may not have been on the menu, but there was definitely plenty of corn, shellfish, squash, and wild game to induce afternoon naps. Thus, a legend was born. Eat, football, sleep, repeat.

Happy Thanksgiving, America!

Thanksgiving

The Pilgrims didn't repeat their feast-bingeing ways the next year, but George Washington, Abraham Lincoln, and Franklin D. Roosevelt all helped bring back the celebration. Washington called for the first Thanksgiving in the newly created United States of America after the Revolutionary War; Lincoln made it a national holiday on the last Thursday in November in order to unite a divided country; Roosevelt wanted to motivate the economy during the Great Depression by making Thanksgiving the fourth Thursday in November. Extra shopping days! The pardoning of turkeys didn't start until George H. W. Bush. Thanks, presidents.

Lived: Nineteenth to twentieth centuries CE, America
Occupation: Abductor on the Underground Railroad, Scout and Spy in the Union Army

Harriet Tubman

Parting the Mason-Dixon Line

Let No Man Stand in Her Way

When Harriet Tubman's master put her up for sale, she prayed that God would change his mind. When that didn't work, she prayed for God to kill him, which happened a week later.

Harriet Tubman felt bad about that, sure, but her master had dug his own grave. He beat Harriet, sometimes on a daily basis, and lent her out to other masters where they could work her to death and beat her, too. Next, he sold two of her sisters down to the Deep South, breaking up Harriet's family.

After her master bit the dust, his widow had a lot of debts to pay. Harriet's family feared they'd all be put up for sale. Their chances of being sold as a package deal were slim-to-fat chance. That's when Harriet and her two brothers hatched a plan to escape.

Unfortunately, her brothers didn't have half the courage Harriet had. While on the run, Harriet's brothers saw their names on a wanted poster. That scared them so badly that they refused to run any farther. It was back to slavery they went and a peeved Harriet decided she had no choice but to follow.

The next time Harriet planned an escape, she decided she would take a different man—her husband, John Tubman. Except he didn't seem to have the courage in him, either. John lived his days as a free black man. Why leave just because his wife had to do back-breaking work from sunup to sundown? His life was fine; he could sleep in on Monday mornings if he wanted.

In Maryland, where they lived, it wasn't unusual for a slave and a freed person to marry. What was unusual was for a free black man to marry a slave woman. According to Maryland law, any kids a woman had took after her. If she was free, they were free. If she was a slave, they were slaves. In other words, any kids John and Harriet had would be slaves like Harriet. He must have liked her, knowing that. Just not enough to escape with her.

When John heard Harriet's plans, he knew trudging through miles of swamps and forests wasn't for him. He may have even threatened to tell her master her plans. Nowadays, it'd be time to call the divorce lawyers, but back then, Harriet gave John the silent treatment and vowed to escape anyway. She was going to be free, and no man would stop her. Not even her husband.

Way Longer Than a Marathon

Harriet Tubman had an abolitionist neighbor. That may sound like a bad skin disease or something worse, but it isn't. Abolitionists wanted to abolish (end) slavery, so Harriet's white neighbor lady gave her directions to a safe house where she could hide. It was one stop on the **Underground Railroad**.

Underground Railroad:

This was a secret network of people, safe houses, and routes that slaves used to escape north. Although it's impossible to know the exact number due to the secret nature of the work they did, the conductors of the Underground Railroad helped thousands of slaves gain their freedom by transporting fugitives from one safe house to another.

A few days after speaking with her neighbor, Harriet left home again, using her wits and the lady's directions to find that first station, which was just somebody's home. The people living there were given cute names like conductors, but they did Houdini-like stuff in order to save their passengers. If they were caught, it meant death for the fugitives they hid and punishment for the conductors, too. During the day, Harriet would do chores for the women of the house in order to look like the help, and at night, the conductors would sneak her to the next stop in the back of a wagon. Then the fugitive would do it all over again.

It definitely wasn't a jog through suburbia to freedom. It was more like running through dense woods and marshes, avoiding snakes and bears, hiding in sacks while bouncing uncomfortably in the backs of wagons, and pretending to still be a slave in order to fool slave catchers. Finally, after almost one hundred miles of running from slave catchers and bloodhounds, she crossed the **Mason-Dixon Line**.

Mason-Dixon Line:

The invisible border separating the North from the South, freedom from slavery.

Harriet was so happy when she crossed the finish line, she thought for a second she might be in heaven. It was only Pennsylvania, but it's an easy mistake when you're excited. Pennsylvania was a free state, so Harriet was finally free, too, as long as she avoided recapture.

Harriet continued to Philadelphia, where she got a job as a dishwasher, cook, or laundress. Her story could have ended here, free at last, but it doesn't because Harriet wasn't content with safety alone. She couldn't shake the fact that her family was still in bondage, and she even missed that annoying husband of hers.

Within a year of her escape to freedom, she made her first trip back to the South. She wanted to help her niece and niece's kids, who were all due to be sold. Somehow, she got messages to her family, possibly through Underground Railroad contacts, and managed to sneak back into Maryland undetected, grab her family members, and make it back to Philadelphia. Or

THREE HUNDRED DOLLARS REWARD.

RANAWAY from the subscriber on Monday the 17th ult., three negroes, named as follows: HARRY, aged about 19 years, has on one side of his neck a wen, just under the ear, he is of a dark chestnut color, about 5 feet 8 or 9 inches hight; BEN, aged aged about 25 years, is very quick to speak when spoken to, he is of a chestnut color, about six feet high; MINTY, aged about 27 years, is of a chestnut color, fine looking, and about 5 feet high. One hundred dollars reward will be given for each of the above named negroes, if taken out of the State, and $50 each if taken in the State. They must be lodged in Baltimore, Easton or Cambridge Jail, in Maryland.

ELIZA ANN BRODESS.

Near Bucktown, Dorchester county, Md.

Oct. 3d, 1849.

☞The Delaware Gazette will please copy the above three weeks, and charge this office.

Minty (Harriet): five feet tall and full of spunk!

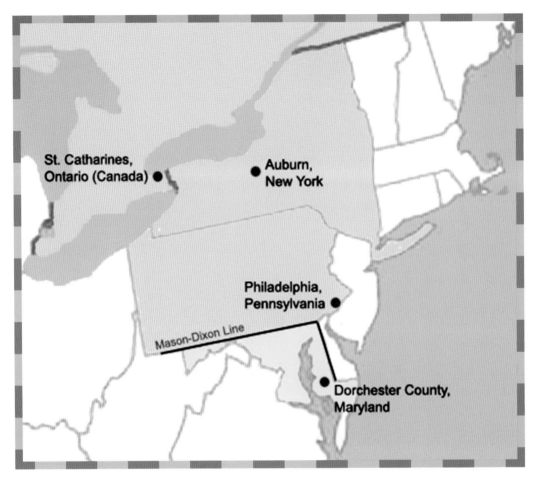

A bunch of important places related to Harriet.

maybe she winged it. Plan or no plan, everything worked out and Harriet determined to keep going back. On her second trip, she brought her brothers with her. (Yes, the two brothers who bailed on her earlier.) On her third trip to Maryland, she tried to get her husband to come, but when she knocked on his door, another woman answered it. That bum had already gotten remarried!

Harriet considered strangling him right then and there, but she thought better of it. Causing a scene isn't the best idea if you're a fugitive. Needless to say, she left John behind for good. His loss. She found other wanna-be fugitives and took them north instead.

It was obvious Harriet was made for this sort of law-breaking, and she became an official **abductor** on the Underground Railroad a year later in

1851. That meant she knew all the safe houses and secret routes on the Railroad, which she used to lead other slaves to freedom.

You know what else she used? Her smarts. Although she never went to school and couldn't read the Wanted Posters with her face plastered on them, she made everyone searching for her look like dumb and dumber.

abductor:

An abductor didn't just conduct fugitives from one house to another; she went to the South to abduct (kidnap) slaves and bring them north. As you might imagine, abductors were rare.

REWARD

$1,000

Who looks stupid now?

Those wanted posters mentioned her illiteracy, so whenever she came across old masters—which happened a lot thanks to always getting "borrowed" out—she hid behind a book or newspaper. It covered her face; plus, no one was looking for a black woman who could read—that would just be weird.

Harriet had other tricks to help her and her escapees along the road, like traveling during the winter because of the longer nights and drugging babies with opium so they would sleep throughout the journey. The opium knocked them clean out. There can't be any crying when you're running for your life.

Harriet Gains a Following

Like a viral video today, Harriet became a celebrity practically **overnight**. She was the breakout pop star of her day, but for different reasons than today's stars. She could have packed out stadiums, too—only her audience would've been grumpy white men who wanted to capture her and collect the reward.

overnight:

Well, over six years and multiple successful runs. But that's pretty good for the 1850s when the quickest way to get information out was the Pony Express—which delivered handwritten mail on horseback.

Harriet Tubman managed to annoy slave masters in three different ways. First, she was a runaway slave. That alone made her a fugitive with a price on her head. Second, she made at least nine trips south as an abductor, leading between two and eleven slaves to freedom each trip. That made her one of the most wanted women in America. Some historians claim that the reward for her capture was as high as $40,000, but that's probably an exaggeration. In any case, a bounty hunter could've gone to Disneyworld on Tubman's reward money, had Disneyworld actually existed back then.

Finally, when she wasn't abducting, Harriet gave speeches and told thrilling stories at abolitionist meetings about her work as an Underground abductor, raising funds and support. She was bringing people to her cause, and that spelled disaster for slavery.

All that buzz inspired a smart white guy to write about Harriet. Franklin B. Sanborn was an abolitionist writer, and for the first time in American history, he mentioned the fact that the history books left out a huge chunk of people—those of African ancestry. He thought that was a shame, since they were worth remembering, too. Harriet certainly accomplished impressive things that needed to be remembered, like never getting caught and never losing a passenger on her many trips back to Maryland.

Part of her success was due to her smarts. The other part was due to her gun. If her brothers taught her anything, it was that people were

How to Be a Fugitive in 1850s America

Harriet Tubman used a number of tactics to get around the South without drawing anyone's attention. Here are a few of her rules for survival:

- Don't leave until Saturday night. No announcement can be placed in the paper until Monday because of the Christian Sabbath.
- Brave the journey during winter when most people want to be inside by their warm fires. Then they won't be out looking for you.
- Go south first. Everyone expects you to head north, so do the opposite!
- Don't act like you own the place. That will draw unwanted attention. Stay small and inconspicuous.
- Know the lingo, including code words, proper knock sequences, and ear lobe tugs. That allows you to communicate with others in the Underground Railroad without ever saying the obvious—"Help, I'm a runaway slave!"

finicky. She already knew that being a fugitive was scary. One minute, her passengers were sneaking through a marsh in the middle of the night, and the next, there's a snake attached to an ankle. Many preferred their straw beds and masters to all that. So Harriet solved the issue by carrying a pistol. If any fugitive changed his mind, she pointed that gun at his head and said, "You'll be free, or dead." That sort of thing tended to motivate a person.

She was right, though. Anyone who turned back endangered the rest of the group. That person could be tortured for information, and if he cracked like an egg once, he could easily crack again. The secrets of the safe houses and the escape routes wouldn't be so secret anymore, and the Underground Railroad would grind to a halt.

Despite the dangers, Harriet kept going back, and it wasn't for the fond childhood memories. Bringing her family out of slavery trumped the risk of recapture. The voices in her head also helped—and they were all thanks to a beating she got as a slave.

There are many versions of this story, but they all end with a white master hitting thirteen-year-old Harriet in the head with a two-pound weight. After the blow, things got a little hairy for Harriet. She started getting visions—strong ones—and they convinced her to save her family. She also had blinding headaches, seizures, and sleeping spells, but that just came with the gig.

Harriet truly believed her visions came from God, and they compelled her to keep going back, even after the federal government acted like a jerk by passing the **Fugitive Slave Act of 1850**.

Fugitive Slave Act of 1850:

A law that allowed all those former slaves who had fled north to freedom to be tracked down, caught, and re-enslaved in the South.

This new law messed up the Railroad's plans. Getting across the Mason-Dixon Line wasn't enough anymore. Harriet and her fellow conductors had to get their passengers all the way to Canada, where slavery was illegal.

Even from Maryland, which isn't exactly the Deep South, it was almost five hundred miles to Ontario, Canada. That's like walking around your block four thousand times!

Now that she was famous, Harriet Tubman split her time between being Moses leading her people to freedom and public speaking engagements. It must have been pretty complicated being a fugitive hiding in the woods one week and the lead speaker at a big event the next. But Harriet figured she should use her celebrity status for good, and her storytelling skills were kind of in demand.

At the public events, she spoke of the cruelty of slavery and the bravery of escaped slaves. She probably didn't talk about the baby drugs, but that's okay. Her talks helped turn many people against the institution of slavery for good.

War

Once the Civil War broke out in 1861, Harriet saw another way to get back at her former masters. She knew that her talents would come in handy, so she volunteered to work for the Union Army.

At first, she did "womanly" things, like cooking and nursing, but her real gift lay in spying. Nobody knew the South better than Harriet, and she wasn't afraid to show up everyone else with her knowledge. Eventually, Union army generals saw how right she was, and they made her a spy and scout.

In the spring of 1863, Harriet was asked to join a raid in South Carolina. She agreed to go under one condition—that Colonel James Montgomery lead the charge. He had been friendly with John Brown, a famous abolitionist, and that was good enough for Harriet. The generals rolled their eyes, but in the end, they agreed to her demands and got down to planning the raid.

The Odd Couple

They say opposites attract, and that's true in the case of Harriet Tubman and John Brown, the crazy abolitionist from Kansas who thought blood and violence was the only way to get anything done.

Back in the 1850s, a black woman and a white man wouldn't normally hang out, but Harriet Tubman and John Brown shared a common bond. They both wanted to end slavery, and they were both willing to take drastic measures to obtain their goal. Harriet swears that she encountered an older white man sporting a white beard in one of her visions. She had no idea what it meant until she met John Brown. His hair wasn't quite white, but it would be soon. All that stress of planning raids and freeing slaves will do that. When John Brown met Harriet, he shook her hand three times and called her "General Tubman." That was enough to make them BFFs. From then on, Harriet helped John Brown raise money and soldiers for his cause. In turn, John always referred to her as "he" or "him," since Harriet was a better man than any of the men he had ever met. (Really, she was just an awesome human being.)

Luckily for Harriet, she fell sick right before John Brown's ill-fated raid on Harper's Ferry, where he was caught, tried, and executed for trying to start a slave uprising. Otherwise, she may have been fighting right next to him and equally tried and executed. Tubman mourned deeply after Brown's death, even naming her beloved hospital project after him—the John Brown Hall. It was eventually renamed the Harriet Tubman Home, but what can you do?

Like a vision—John Brown's mesmerizing grizzled face.

The Union army's goal was to disarm mines set by the Confederates along the Combahee (pronounced KUM-bee) River. They also planned to blow up bridges and railroad tracks in the area in order to disrupt supply lines and to generally wreak havoc. It seemed like a suicide mission, but, hey, what wasn't during war?

In the end, the good outweighed the risks. Plus, the raid would be a great opportunity for Harriet to free as many slaves as possible. The **Emancipation Proclamation** had been issued by President Abraham Lincoln, but plantation owners didn't seem to get the message. So Harriet decided to help show them what they were supposed to do.

During the South Carolina raid, Harriet had to convince the nervous slaves she was trying to liberate that the ironclad gunboats were safe to jump aboard. At first, the slaves thought she'd listened to those voices for too long, but once they realized the gunboats weren't iron alligators or sinking death traps, they hopped aboard. Not even threats from plantation owners could stop them. The soldiers finished it all off by burning the planta-

Emancipation Proclamation:

A speech given on January 1, 1863, by President Abraham Lincoln proclaiming the freedom of slaves, but only in rebelling states. It didn't end slavery or even outlaw it in all states, yet the proclamation changed the feeling of the war. Now, it was about more than keeping the Union together. It was about freedom—if the Union won, that is. Slavery wasn't officially abolished until 1865 with the passing of the Thirteenth Amendment.

Iron monsters on a river.

tions to the ground, effectively cutting off more crops and food supplies for the South and its army. The raid was a complete victory with more than seven hundred slaves freed, not to mention whatever goods they could carry—like armfuls of chickens and bags of piglets. Essentials.

Harriet spent the rest of the war (until 1865) doing her thing—bribing people for information, scouting good locations for raids, and wiping gore off wounded soldiers that would make most people vomit. Only a cape could complete her Superwoman act.

The Good Ole Days Are Over

It's not often that war and slavery are the high points of a person's life, but that might have been the case for poor Harriet Tubman. After the Civil War ended and slavery was officially over, things kind of went downhill for the rebel.

Despite becoming a huge celebrity—Queen Victoria invited Harriet to her birthday party in England—Harriet's skills as an Underground Railroad abductor and Union spy didn't do her much good anymore. On a train ride

Show me the money.

bogus:

For years, Harriet fought to get her back pay, and after the intervention of a bunch of bankers and lawyers, she was finally awarded twelve dollars a month for being a nurse, eight dollars a month for being a widow of a soldier, and five hundred 'we're sorry" dollars. It still didn't cover what she should have made as a scout and spy.

to her home in Auburn, New York, Harriet figured her government service entitled her to sit wherever she wanted like it did for other soldiers. The white train conductor didn't agree and he threw her from the car into baggage. When Harriet tried to fight back, she managed to break a few of her own ribs, but that was it.

Then there was the problem of her pay. For three years of service to the Union Army as a nurse, cook, and commander of scouts, she only received two hundred dollars. That was like earning three cents an hour, which was totally **bogus**! Although she was swindled out of much of her pay, Harriet remained true to her giving nature, and she used the money to build a house where she taught newly freed women how to wash laundry for wages.

To make matters worse, Harriet had a lot of mouths to feed, including her family and many former Underground escapees who needed a place to crash now that they were in the North without a home.

What money and goods Harriet did have, she eventually lost. Her house burned down and multiple scam artists swindled her right into poverty five years after the war. Even her rent-paying pigs died on the little farm she was building. To get by, Harriet took in boarders, which is how she met her second husband. Unfortunately, he had tuberculosis and died in 1888. Harriet couldn't catch a break.

She did have one last run in her, though. Her dream was to build a hospital for African Americans where the orphaned and elderly could be safe and cared for. To raise money for such a place, Harriet joined forces with famous suffragists committed to women's right to vote. These were women like Susan B. Anthony, who you may know from the silver dollar.

Harriet went to suffragist meetings and spoke about the adventures she and other women in the anti-slavery movement had experienced. She talked about the hardships they all endured and the challenges they overcame. Although her talks weren't directly about women's voting rights, suffragists

Harriet Tubman Home: now I'm a tourist attraction!

vote:

Apparently not, since women didn't get the right to vote in the United States until 1920.

saw Harriet's point—if women can do all this, don't you think they should be able to **vote**?

Eventually, Harriet grew so old that she had to move into the hospital she helped build. There, she died of pneumonia in 1913. She'd outlived slavery, war, and two husbands to become one of the most important fugitives in US history. The fight for equal rights for both women and African Americans would continue long past her death, but so would Harriet's legacy. She became the poster child for courage under fire. People recognized her daring and generosity, and so the legend of Harriet Tubman began.

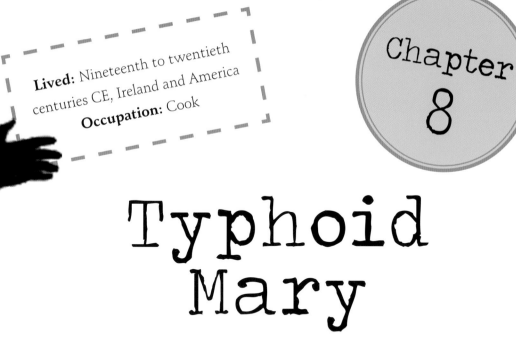

Chapter 8

Lived: Nineteenth to twentieth centuries CE, Ireland and America
Occupation: Cook

Typhoid Mary

Killer Cook

Time to Order Take-Out

When you think of death by disease today, typhoid fever doesn't usually spring to mind, but it did in 1906. It took unsuspecting victims by the intestine and made them diarrhea themselves to death, among other nasty complications. Typhoid fever is caused by Salmonella Typhi, a rod-shaped bacterium that passes from human to human via urine or feces, which means an infected person probably ate bits of poop at some point. And it only took one infected pooping person to start an epidemic.

In 1900, typhoid was one of the top five fatal infectious diseases in America. So when people found out that a woman could carry typhoid fever for life and never get sick (called a **healthy carrier**), they were

healthy carrier: Someone who has a disease and can pass it on to others, but never has the symptoms themselves.

ready to skewer her like a kebob. It was either that or let her kill everyone in sight with the deadly disease.

Mary Mallon was a woman who just wanted to cook, but her poop-contaminated hands doomed her and tens of others. Yes, tens.

When disease detectives finally tracked Mary down, the story of the killer cook spread like the plague. Mary Mallon was now known as Typhoid Mary, the kitchen killer. Lock up your dish pans and break your wooden spoons, Mary was out to get you!

Moving On Up

Mary Mallon was born in Ireland shortly after the Great Potato Famine of the late 1840s had wreaked death and destruction throughout the country. As you might have guessed, there was nothing great about starving to death and eating teeny, tiny diseased potatoes with your fingers morning, noon, and night. Officially, the famine had ended by the time of Mary's birth, but it was still affecting families. Like millions of others between 1845 and 1910, Mary left that misery behind and immigrated to New York. She went by herself at the age of fourteen, because that's the way Mary did things—courageously and alone.

Things were pretty bad in 1880s New York for the newly landed Irish immigrants. Most lived in tenements, which were foul places to take a stroll and fouler places to live. People slogged through tons of horse and human waste in the streets, as well as uncollected garbage and dead animal bodies every day. No one thought to scoop the poop even though they all knew it was bad for people's health. Some people still thought the rampant diseases were coming from the bad smells (they called it miasma), but at least they knew the poo was a problem. No one with real power wanted to step up to fix things. If they got too close, they might get sick.

Luckily for Mary, she had a talent, and it was her ticket to the good life in her new city. She was a cook and a pretty awesome one at that. Her signature dish was peaches and cream. Those hoity-toity rich people couldn't get enough of her luscious peaches, so she kept getting jobs as an in-home chef with various upscale employers. These jobs paid way more than schlepping dirty laundry or cleaning all day, and the work wasn't nearly as back breaking.

Home Sweet Toilet

Mary practically became a member of the families she worked for, even going on trips to their fancy beach homes to cook for them during summer vacations. Mary had climbed from the lowest rung of society to somewhere in the middle, all by herself. Now she stayed in the same neighborhoods as **presidents**!

When her new employers' families came down with typhoid fever, as they almost all did, Mary sometimes helped nurse them. Mary believed she was indispensable, except she wasn't.

Elementary, Dear Watson

Mary didn't seem to notice that every family she worked for came down with raging fevers after eating her finger-licking good

presidents:

Teddy Roosevelt, the twenty-sixth US president, had a vacation home in Oyster Bay, one of the neighborhoods Mary worked in, and he stayed there so much during his presidency (1901 to 1909), it was called the "Summer White House."

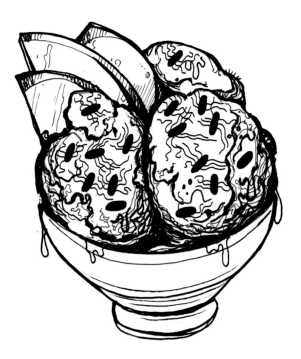

Does that come in other flavors?

peaches and cream special. (Or did she?) In fact, no one connected the dots until one sanitary engineer named George Soper came along.

Maybe Soper had read too many Sherlock Holmes novels, because he fancied himself a detective—a disease detective. That's the way he billed himself to all the fancy folk, at least. He helped clean up cities after natural disasters by keeping them sanitary, and he was gaining a reputation as a good-looking expert in mopping up the deadly, typhoid fever–causing bacteria, too. One sick family in Oyster Bay hired Soper to investigate the illness, because wealthy people didn't catch typhoid fever. It was a disease for the poor masses in dirty, poo-filled slums, not for bankers and presidents.

George Soper rode to the rescue. He pulled out his detective cap and got to work, checking the drinking water, the toilets, and the bay where fresh oysters were collected. (Well, what did you think the name was for?) He found nothing. Usually feces in a water well was a good guess, but he couldn't find so much as a brown trace. Things were not going well for the detective.

At this point, Soper may have been asking himself, *What would Sherlock Holmes do?* Then it came to him: work backwards! Maybe it was a person passing the disease along. So Soper questioned everyone from the milkman to the family dog, hoping to track down the culprit.

Then it happened: a stroke of luck, a lightning strike twice in the same place, a muddy paw print next to the empty plate of ham. Soper found out the cook the family had hired for the summer had recently disappeared without a trace, right after their fevers hit. Bingo!

Demon in Disguise

Soper felt it was his duty to protect the good (rich) people of Oyster Bay—nay, the world—from this terrible disease and its carrier. He needed to track down this cook. For the next few months, Soper pulled out his magnifying glass and searched high and low for any trace of the missing woman by contacting her employment agency.

Although he didn't find her, he did find a pattern. Apparently, outbreaks followed her, and once they struck, she had the bad habit of quitting. Or smart habit. Either way, it looked suspicious. Obviously, she considered her work done once the disease was present in her current family, and then she moved on to the next victim. Soper would find her, though. He hadn't become a disease detective for nothing. The clues were all leading him to the same conclusion about his mystery cook—she was America's first healthy carrier of typhoid fever.

It was a hunch at this point, but one that could launch Soper to fame and fortune. Recently, the famous bacteriologist Robert Koch had identified the first healthy carrier of typhoid fever in Germany. Germany had named an **award** after Koch, they were so thankful for his discovery. If it had made Koch a celebrity in Germany, think of the career-making discovery this would be for Soper!

award:
The award money was given through a foundation to researchers. Not only was the foundation named after Koch, but then they awarded him the first prize money for his tuberculosis research, which proved tuberculosis wasn't genetic. Koch also worked with the nasty little buggers (bacteria) causing anthrax and cholera, but Soper had to start somewhere!

At least, that's how Soper thought about it. He could already see it: National George Soper Day had a nice ring to it.

It took one more typhoid fever episode for Soper to track down his woman. This time, the outbreak was on swanky Park Avenue in New York City. Lady Luck was with Soper, because when he knocked on the door, he found the diseased demon-in-disguise cooking.

All Soper had to do was explain to Mary that she was killing the young woman dying of typhoid fever upstairs and that he'd need to take blood, feces, and urine samples to make sure he was right. As you might expect, this didn't go over as well as he had hoped. Mary couldn't believe what he was telling her: invisible germs in her not-sick body were killing the family she cared for? Pshaw. They had the wrong woman. She'd never been sick a day in her life.

To Soper, there was only one explanation for Mary's denial—she knew she was a human petri dish, and she was out for blood. Whatever her true motive was, Mary reacted to his accusation by waving a carving fork around and chasing Soper out the door, yelling not-so-nice things the whole way.

Like any good detective, Soper began digging around for dirt on his suspect. He found Mary's live-in-boyfriend and made him spill his guts. From the boyfriend, Soper discovered where Mary's apartment was and what time she'd be home. Then he went to the address to wait for her.

This was so going to work.

The Most Dangerous Woman in America

Mary didn't exactly appreciate being followed around like a common criminal. This guy clearly judged her for being an unmarried, working-class immigrant and for being a woman, given the way he treated her as if she were an idiot. It only took one look at the skinny, rat-faced man accusing her of being a disease carrier in her own home for Mary to want him gone. She yelled about how clean she was and told him about the time she nursed a sick family at her own risk.

Not looking forward to another encounter with Mary's large, pointy weapon of choice, Soper decided to leave while he still had all his body parts and turned the case over to the **NYC Health Department**.

The NYC Health Department officials decided a female doctor might calm down the scrappy Irishwoman. But just in case, they also sent a horse-drawn ambulance and five policemen to force Mary to come with them. If SWAT teams had existed in 1907, they might have sent one of those, too. They were treating Mary like she was a walking epidemic or something.

Dr. Sara Josephine Baker tried talking Mary into coming with her, but the cook wasn't going down easy. Like a hunted animal, Mary fled the kitchen with a carving fork for protection. Dr. Baker had the police spread out around the building while she shook down the servants for information on Mary's whereabouts. That was a dead end, though, because the staff had more loyalty to Mary than people expected. It was a lot of "Mary who?" when they were asked for information. The doctor couldn't get a thing out of them.

NYC Health Department:

The New York City Health Department started recording infectious diseases in 1796, but it wasn't until 1866 that they gained any real power to combat diseases. Now, the department could vaccinate people and set up sewer systems instead of just taking notes. In 1892, New York set up the country's first bacterial lab for the health of the public after a cholera outbreak. Then the city's government decided to keep it open after they realized diseases weren't going away. *Ever.*

Three hours later, Dr. Baker was ready to give up, but her boss made it clear she must bring in Mary or else. After another two hours of searching for the fugitive, the police found Mary curled up in a neighbor's tiny, dark closet—she'd even scaled a fence in a dress and apron to escape. They dragged her out kicking, screaming, and punching. Dr. Baker had to sit on Mary during the entire ambulance ride to the hospital to keep her detained.

When Mary's lab tests came back, it confirmed all suspicions. Mary was the first healthy carrier of typhoid discovered in America, making her the Most Dangerous Woman in the country. When the media got wind of it, Mary's fate was sealed. No one wanted a killer cook on the loose, especially not a violent Irish one. She was dubbed Typhoid Mary, and she'd never live it down. In fact, that same nickname is still used a hundred years later to describe anyone who passes any disease to another, knowingly or not.

What happened next could be straight out of a nightmare, but it wasn't. It was just Mary Mallon's life.

You won't take me alive!

Stubborn as a Mule

Some of this was Mary's fault. She wasn't what you'd call a "people person." Her voice was loud, and a lot of the words that came out of it would make your grandma gasp. In Mary's defense, no one was explaining things to her. She was told she must have had typhoid fever, gotten over it, and become immune. Doctors also told her they wanted to take out her **gall bladder** to cure her.

gall bladder:

Removing one's gall bladder was one of the ways doctors of the day thought they could cure healthy typhoid carriers, not that it worked. Of the five healthy carriers doctors talked into surgery, all of them still carried typhoid after the gall bladder's removal.

Mary trusted the doctors and Soper about as much as she trusted the potato crops in Ireland, which wasn't much. She doubted anyone would care if the scalpel

Scrambled eggs, anyone?

happened to slip during surgery. She'd be one less poor immigrant to worry about in a city teeming with them. No, thank you.

Since she refused surgery, the NYC Board of Health marooned her on an island filled with a bunch of highly contagious, disease-ridden tuberculosis patients, and let her think about what she'd done. People were sent there to die. She did get her own extremely lonely cottage on the island. It was the least they could do.

A few scientists objected, but the health department put its foot down. The city couldn't jeopardize the health of many for the freedom of one. After her transport to the tuberculosis island, doctors started trying out experimental drugs on Mary, to see if they could find a cure for the disease she refused to believe she carried.

For the next two years, Mary stayed put with only a dog as her companion. Sometimes, her captors let her boyfriend visit. Most of the time she stayed in her cottage writing angry letters about how she wasn't sick and wanted to

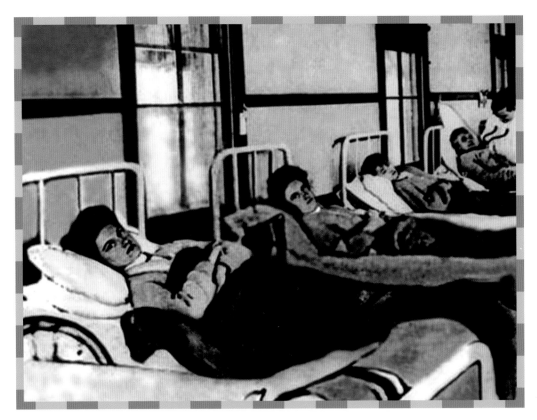

Mary in bed: But I feel fine!

go home. She hired a lawyer who agreed with her. Where was Mary's justice? There had been no trial, no judge, nothing before the city **quarantined** her. The public lapped up the story like chocolate milk.

Finally, Mary got her day in court. It didn't help. The old men of the Supreme Court, the highest law of the land, looked at her like they would a giant squid in the open ocean—terrified. Despite fifty other cases of **healthy carriers** that had been discovered, she was the only one locked up, because she was the only one who was a cook. Typhoid fever typically passes through fecal matter and urine, and when Mary made her peaches and cream special, she clearly hadn't been washing her hands well enough. Scrub-a-dub-dub under those nails like you're going into surgery. She was also a woman, so health officials didn't find it as necessary to help her find meaningful work. She wasn't a breadwinner in their eyes. When Typhoid Tony, another cook, was found to be a healthy carrier, officials gave him a good job because he was a breadwinner. It was Mary's bad luck to be born a girl.

Instead of making a better effort to help her, the court and the Health Department asked Mary if she would leave New York; that way she'd be another state's **problem**. Mary

quarantined:

Isolating sick people or anyone who is exposed to sickness to help stop the spread of diseases. Quarantines were first used by the US Federal Government to stop yellow fever from spreading in 1878, but the American colonies and states had quarantined people before that.

healthy carriers:

Three percent of people who recover from typhoid fever become healthy carriers.

problem:

Just tell them you're going to live with your "sister" in Connecticut. (She didn't have a sister.) One guy asked the health department to sneak Mary into Michigan so he could marry her. He believed a good cook was the best quality in a wife. He also mentioned he had been certified insane for a bit but that was three years ago. He almost got his way until his neighbors objected to Mary's presence for some reason, and he was declined the offer.

refused. Even killer cooks have principles, and she'd always been a stubborn lady.

It would take a new guy in charge at the Health Department to get Mary released after three years. Dr. Ernest Lederle didn't see how the city could exile all those healthy carriers, so he made Mary promise to stop being a cook and to check in with the Health Department every month for an examination. Then he found her a job as a laundry lady, which was a *gigantic* step down from being a cook. It wasn't like employers were jumping up and down to hire her, so she grudgingly took the lower status job.

Life stunk, and she hated doing laundry. Mary tried suing anyone she could think of after her release, but it didn't help. Eventually, she shook off parole and went on the run under an assumed name: Mary Brown. Finally, she could cook again. Typhoid Mary was back in business.

The Jig Is Up

Mary still bounced from scummy job to scummy job for five years, angry and annoyed. Now, she was slinging slop, rather than getting her just desserts in ritzy New York brownstones (old fancy homes). So maybe she didn't care anymore if the typhoid thing was true. Or maybe she really didn't believe those haughty doctors who had locked her up for years. She'd given samples to an independent lab to prove she didn't have any disease—and they came back **negative** for typhoid. Those quacks at the NYC Health Department had to be wrong.

All seemed settled until another outbreak of typhoid occurred in a place where Mary was cooking. The Health Department was notified of a typhoid outbreak at a maternity hospital, and when they went to investigate, it became all too clear another cook was behind the disease. Another cook named

negative:

It's possible all those negative results had been mishandled or were collected on a day when Mary wasn't shedding bacteria. The disease wasn't present in her poop every day, which is why only seven out of eight families that Soper traced to Mary had gotten sick.

Mary, no less, who had quit after the outbreak. They even traced the origins back to pudding. It was practically Mary's MO. Officials realized Mary Brown was Mary Mallon, the real life Typhoid Mary. (Both Baker and Soper claimed credit for identifying her.)

A friend ratted out Mary to the investigators, telling them when Mary would visit next. There, they cornered the cook in a bathroom and arrested her. Mary didn't so much as squeak, let alone try to punch anyone's nose in this time. She was getting old, and it was hard to deny the facts anymore.

It was back to the island for her. North Brother Island wasn't a lifelong vacation to the Bahamas, but she had sealed her fate with the last outbreak, which had caused two deaths. She had no choice. Like usual, she was alone. Her boyfriend had died of heart disease and the friendly lawyer of tuberculosis. Even worse, the newspapers were no longer sympathetic to her cause. Everyone in America condemned Mary for cooking again.

Mary incubated typhoid in her body until the day she died from pneumonia, twenty-three years later. She refused to talk about typhoid and became Hulk-like if anyone brought up the health department charlatans. (That

Not exactly paradise.

didn't stop her fellow castaways from calling her Typhoid Mary behind her back.)

So what was Mary's total death count? Three documented deaths and forty-seven people sickened. There might have been more unconnected incidents before she became Typhoid Mary, although that's something we'll never know for sure.

It would be another ten years before there were antibiotics to treat typhoid fever victims. Mary was doomed from the start, but her story helped to prove it wasn't smells and miasma that caused disease. People could carry it, too.

communicable disease:

A sickness that's passable from a contagious person or animal.

Today, typhoid fever still exists. An outbreak in 2010 infected twelve people after they ate bacteria-laced fruit smoothies in America; however, typhoid is more common in developing countries with poor water supplies. In 2015, Uganda announced over a thousand confirmed cases of typhoid fever with thousands more suspected.

Today, people suspected of being sick with a **communicable disease** can expect similar isolation pro-

Healthy Hazard

Mary wasn't your typical fugitive on the run, but the ramifications of tracking her down and isolating her still affect us today. We still ask ourselves these questions: Should we separate people who are sick? How sick do they have to be? For how long should they be isolated from society?

Laws today allow the detainment of anyone who is "suspected of carrying a communicable disease." No one's going to be knocking down your door in a hazmat suit if you get chicken pox, but you could be isolated for diseases including typhoid fever, influenza, tuberculosis, plague, smallpox, yellow fever, Ebola, and SARS. Just like they did to Mary Mallon, health officials can isolate you from the world until they decide you're safe. Most modern quarantines only last as long as absolutely necessary, which can be anywhere from a few hours to a few weeks. Breaking quarantine in most states is a criminal act. But what should be done with people like Mary, who are healthy hazards?

Today, health officials believe healthy carriers need to be made aware of healthy living practices and taught how they can prevent the spread of disease. They need to be able to trust that their government won't discriminate against them like what happened in Mary's case. The best way to do this is still up for debate.

cedures—for a little while. Health departments have the important job of protecting the rest of the public from contagious outbreaks, and they have lots of power to get that job done. For example, the current quarantine time in the United States for Ebola is twenty-one days, proving the story of Mary Mallon is a lot more relevant than you'd think.

You Decide:

What is more important: your rights or your health?

Chapter 9

Lived: Twentieth century CE, America
Occupation: Bank robber

John Dillinger

Not Exactly Robin Hood

Real Life Cops and Robbers

Some kids dream about becoming a doctor, a teacher, or a super-cool spy when they grow up. Not John Dillinger. In fact, spies were pretty scary to him. That's because he wanted to get rich quick and not in the traditional way. Robbery was more his style.

Dillinger teamed up with the likes of Baby Face Nelson and Machine Gun Kelly to steal from the rich in order to give to themselves. It only took one spectacular year of running around robbing banks, escaping jail cells, and outracing police cars before Dillinger became America's first Public Enemy Number One.

It should come as no surprise that Dillinger spent most of his life as a fugitive or behind bars before dying in a gunfight at age thirty-one. Despite all that delinquency and law breaking, he managed to give America one important thing—the Federal Bureau of Investigation. Yes, the FBI was formed thanks to one really bad egg.

A Life on the Run

Usually, the truth isn't as exciting as Hollywood cops and robbers stories, but that wasn't the case with John Dillinger. It's almost as if Dillinger's dream was to become a fugitive. He didn't waste any time, at least. By nineteen, he'd stolen his first car, panicked, slipped out of a policeman's grip, and ran away to join the navy.

It only took a few weeks for Dillinger to realize honest work was for chumps. He hated shoveling coal into hot burners all day, and it made his hands all calloused and gross. So he slipped off the boat for a day of unauthorized fun. This didn't go over well with his superiors, and it led to a month of getting in trouble, being thrown in the brig, rebelling, getting into more trouble, and, finally, escaping the navy altogether.

The navy probably breathed a sigh of relief when he left, but they tacked a fifty-dollar reward on his head for abandoning his duty, anyway. Eventually, this would be small beans compared to the bounty the founder of the FBI, J. Edgar Hoover, would offer for that same head a few years later.

You'd think that with two fugitive statuses under his belt Dillinger would slow down a little. Not a chance. Shortly after he escaped from the navy, an ex-convict taught Dillinger how to rob weakling old men. It should have been easier than taking candy from a baby, but the first old man he targeted fought back. Dillinger may have had a metal bar, but he still ended up in handcuffs.

Despite it technically being his first offense, the judge threw the book at him. The Navy didn't want him back, either. They **dishonorably discharged** him, which is typically done when someone commits a serious crime.

Without a lawyer to help talk him up, Dillinger got ten to twenty. This time, there was no slipping out of a policeman's grip. He spent the next nine years making shirts in prison before getting parole. Being in prison was like being in college—except the degree was in law-breaking.

dishonorably discharged:

This release from the military also releases the person from benefits, including pay and honor, and it can follow a person forever, making it hard to find a job or bank loan, and making it easy for society to shun him.

Congrats, Graduate!

Dillinger hardened up while in jail, made a bunch of convict friends, like Henry Pierpont, and formed a life plan. It wasn't too complex; he wanted to rob as many banks as possible and to have lots of fast cars and money.

Easy, right? A little too easy.

Jackrabbited

In the 1920s and '30s, banks were pretty much asking to be robbed. It wasn't a federal offense to rob a bank, and most of the time, nobody put up a fight if someone strolled up to a teller and demanded all the cash in the drawer. Even your grandma could hobble out of the bank faster than it took local police to respond. In fact, Indiana's state police, where Dillinger lived and stole, started up the same time as Dillinger did—they were practically twins! Since local law enforcement was still in its infancy, bank robbers had the run of towns.

It didn't help that guns were almost easier to find than food. In order to buy a submachine gun in Dillinger's day, all he needed to do was plunk down some money on a gun dealer's counter and walk out of the store, no questions asked. But he decided that paying for guns wasn't good for his wallet, especially when all it took to get them for free was a little courage.

With his gang in tow, Dillinger would run into a police station, demand all the weapons, and race out again. It sounds ridiculously suicidal today, but in the '30s, police stations weren't highly guarded forts with trained specialists—at least, not yet. Dillinger's antics would change all that. Shortly after

No one wants to stand in the cold for hours to get some coffee.

Dillinger started living his life of crime, police demanded faster cars and bulletproof vests to match the outlaws' getup.

It also helped his cause that the people wanted him to beat the banks. The 1920s might have roared with prosperity and parties, but they led to the 1930s, which just meowed pitifully. That's because the Great Depression struck America after the stock market crash in 1929. Millions of people were out of jobs, and they were hungry and worried. Lots of banks shut down, taking the hard-earned money of their customers with them. In many people's eyes, banks ranked up there with homework on weekends—pure evil. Lots of robbers stole straight from bank vaults, pretending to be modern-day **Robin Hoods**, and the public loved it.

Robin Hoods:

Except these crooks mostly kept their ill-gotten gains for themselves, unlike Robin Hood who (allegedly) gave to the poor. The public still hero-worshipped them, though.

I should be made into a comic book superhero! Or villain. Whatever.

In a few months, Dillinger made up for all that lost time in jail. While relieving banks of their cash and diamonds, he also perfected his signature move, because every supervillain needs a calling card. During his stickups, Dillinger would bounce over bank counters like he had springs glued to his feet, so everyone called him Jackrabbit. He loved it.

Soon, Dillinger had thousands of dollars, guns, and a budding gang. The only problem were his friends. They were still behind bars. But Dillinger had a plan to break them out of jail. Unfortunately for Dillinger, he also had a very determined police officer on his trail. Matt Leach, captain of the Indiana State Police, didn't take the convict's string of robberies sitting down. He chased Dillinger all over Indiana, but always arrived a day late and a few thousand dollars short.

Dillinger was so confident that Leach couldn't catch him that he would call Leach on the telephone to taunt him. He even sent him a book: *How To Be a Detective*. Ouch.

In return, livid Leach pinned almost every **criminal event** in Indiana on Dillinger, whether he had actually committed the crime or not.

As fun as taunting Leach and robbing banks were, even a fugitive needs a day off before a big job. Dillinger spent his in Chicago at the World's Fair, snapping pictures of police officers, confident that they could never catch him. And he was right.

criminal event:
Dillinger joked that Leach would accuse him of murdering Abe Lincoln next, who had been dead for more than sixty years.

Instead, Dillinger was caught by detectives in Dayton, Ohio, in September 1933. The Dayton detectives found a suspiciously detailed map of his friends' prison in Dillinger's pocket. Dillinger played dumb, and the detectives didn't do anything smart, like tell the prison.

This was a bad idea, since Dillinger had already smuggled the map and guns to his friends before he was arrested. Pierpont and his gang split from the joint a few days later. It was the largest prison break in Indiana history. There must have been some honor in thieves since Pierpont returned the favor. After getting wheels, guns, and robbing a bank of ten thousand dollars, he busted Dillinger out of jail, too.

Pierpont and his gang came to the jail dressed as cops and wanted to see Dillinger. When the sheriff asked to see their credentials, they showed him their guns. That got their message across, but they didn't stop there. Pierpont shot and killed the sheriff before strolling into the tiny jail and unlocking Dillinger's cell himself.

Over the next few months, the gang really got on a roll, robbing banks, killing cops, and barging into police stations demanding guns like they owned the world. When anyone pursued them, the fugitives dropped buckets of nails on the road from their faster cars and laughed all the way to their hideout. Still, it wasn't enough to get federal agents involved.

J. Edgar Hoover wasn't a sleep-in-and-make-pancakes type. He hated sitting back and waiting while crimes happened all over the country, but, back then, there wasn't a lot a criminal could do to get busted by the feds. According to the laws of the time, in order to get the big guys involved, a person had to blow up a national park, commit treason, or cross a state line with a stolen car. That sort of thing.

So Hoover waited for an opportunity to get in on the chase. He was tired of criminals like Dillinger doing bad stuff, then **escaping** into another state to avoid the law, and he had just the plan to stop it.

Dillinger wasn't in the blowing up national parks business, but he did enjoy stealing cars.

Shh, I'm Hunting Wabbits

After a long winter of robbing banks and vacationing in Florida, Dillinger became a celebrity. He was **"Public Enemy No. 1"** in Illinois, and all top ten spots were taken by members of his gang. There was now a Chicago task force called the Dillinger Squad, established to capture the criminal. Dillinger loved the attention. If there was a newspaper clipping about him, Dillinger would spend hours admiring the story. Everything was coming up Dillinger. Until he got caught, again.

This time, Dillinger was in Arizona, but Captain Leach quickly got him sent back to Indiana to face previous murder charges. Dillinger was placed in the "escape-proof cell," which meant it took Dillinger a month to hoof it out of there. Some say he whittled a fake gun out of wood and blackened it with shoe polish to trick the guards into thinking he had a real gun. Others are convinced a few Ben Franklins greased the guards' hands. Either way, Dillinger escaped, stole the **sheriff's car**, and crossed the state line into Illinois.

Despite highway blockades, police raids, and twenty thousand people looking for one guy, Dillinger disappeared into the countryside like a wild goose leading everyone on a chase. Even though there was a dangerous criminal on the loose, Hoover probably felt as giddy as a schoolgirl. Robbing banks might not be a federal offense, but crossing a state line with a stolen car definitely was. Using Dillinger as his platform, Hoover called for a more active federal role in law enforcement.

Dillinger's celebrity star was about to become brighter. Hoover crowned him America's first Public Enemy Number One. Then Hoover put up reward posters all over the country and started assigning "special agents" to specific cases, including a whole team of special agents to Dillinger's case. These special agents were called **G-Men**.

Bohemian Tragedy

Actually, the whole 'waiting until Dillinger crossed the state lines" story may be just that: a story. Hoover wanted to seem like a cool, calm superhero to the public, but this wasn't the first time he tried to catch the Jackrabbit. The first time was in Wisconsin in April of 1934. Dillinger and the gang (including Baby Face Nelson, a shoot first, never ask questions kind of guy) were holed up in a lodge in Little Bohemia for another vacation. Under the cover of darkness, Agent Purvis and his men inched closer to the cabin, disturbing a bunch of dogs with their not-so-subtle approach.

That wasn't enough to get Dillinger out of bed, but when the agents accidentally shot an innocent civilian staying at the lodge, he was up and at 'em. There was more shooting, an agent was killed, and Dillinger's whole gang escaped. That didn't make Hoover or his agents look too great, so he covered it up and waited for the Jackrabbit to make another fatal mistake—crossing state lines.

sheriff's car:

Sheriff Holley was not impressed. She wanted to track Dillinger down and shoot him herself.

G-Men:

Short for government men. The nickname, embraced by Hoover, started thanks to Machine Gun Kelly. In a tight situation, Kelly came out with his hands up, yelling for the G-Men not to shoot him.

I'm having too much fun to hide.

Hoover convinced politicians to give his agents the right to carry weapons and to arrest people who they believed were connected with federal crimes. Congress started a war on thieves and made a lot more **crimes** federal offenses. They passed ten new laws called the "New Deal on Crime," claiming that people like Dillinger made these laws necessary. Then, Hoover sent his agents into the field to catch those felons. As Dillinger's celebrity rose higher, so did Hoover's. Now Hoover needed to catch Dillinger quickly, before politicians decided the G-men were a waste of money.

> **crimes:**
>
> Robbing banks, kidnapping, killing a fed, committing crimes over state lines, stealing cars . . . all things bad guys like to do.

Don't Trust a Lady in Orangish-Red

Dillinger knew Hoover was on to him. It wasn't hard to figure out when he saw his face plastered all over town with a **$10,000 reward** beneath his mugshot. The way Dillinger saw it, he had to change his face.

> **$10,000 reward:**
>
> That's five times what a family would make in a year during the Great Depression.

Radical? Maybe. Dillinger got plastic surgery and sauntered around big cities like Chicago, practically begging the police to catch him. He'd go to Cubs games and movie theaters, walking in plain daylight with no fear. It was fun to smile at cops as he passed and way better than hiding in a hole like some scared rabbit. Although it wasn't the smartest plan a fugitive has ever had.

The only way the agents were sure they'd catch Dillinger was if someone betrayed him. A special agent assigned to his case, Melvin Purvis, decided to do just that. Of course, he'd need somebody else close to Dillinger to do the actual betraying. Preferably a woman. Being the stud muffin Dillinger thought he was, he'd never expect a beautiful girl to betray him. Didn't all the ladies love him?

Not Anna Sage. Born in Romania, she faced deportation on account of her being a foreigner with "low morals." When she found out her new friend

Should have stayed in and read a book.

was actually John Dillinger, she saw dollar signs and much more—her ticket to stay in America.

Negotiations weren't Anna's strong suit, and all Agent Purvis agreed to do in return for her help in capturing Dillinger was to *try* to stop the government from kicking her out of the country. *Maybe* she'd get a percentage of the reward money, too. Clearly desperate, Anna agreed.

On Sunday, July 22, 1934, Anna called the feds. She let Agent Purvis know that she, another woman, and Dillinger were headed to the movies and that she'd be wearing a bright orange skirt as her signal. Then the three amigos went to the Biograph Theater in Chicago and laughed through a romantic comedy.

Just kidding. They saw *Manhattan Melodrama*, a gangster movie. Well, what else would a gangster want to see? Yes, Dillinger was having a good day. He was arm in arm with two ladies and still outwitting the cops. Then he exited the theater and noticed a bunch of nervous-looking men around. At that point, it was adios, ladies. Dillinger dropped their arms and scampered into a nearby alley. Hoover's men were all over, though. Six bangs later and the Jackrabbit was dead, shot through the eye.

Hoover must have been ecstatic. Anna's dress color became red in the retellings, and she became the famous "Lady in Red." She received $5,000 as a reward. She also was deported. Even the good guys aren't perfect.

Finally Giving Back

Everyone wanted a piece of the gangster once he was dead. Thousands went to view his body, entrepreneurs dipped handkerchiefs in his blood to sell for a hefty profit, and plaster masks were made of his face. Hoover kept one of the masks around the office as a memento and to scare troublemaker kids. Doctors also removed Dillinger's brain so they could figure out where it all went wrong for the Jackrabbit. Unfortunately for science, it was stolen before any mysteries could be figured out.

Even the coroners got in on the business of Dillinger's death. They'd label a toe tag with his name, drape it around his big toe for a few seconds, and then sell it as a souvenir.

Dillinger died at thirty-one years of age after a fourteen-month reign of terror. He supposedly had wads of

Here's Who Has 'Em

Fancy looking onto the face of the Jackrabbit in person? You're in luck. Dillinger's death masks are still preserved and on display in various places around the country.

Two of the four masks are in private collections, but they sometimes travel in special exhibits to museums. The other two are at the Chicago History Museum in Chicago, Illinois, and at the National Museum of Crime and Punishment in Washington, DC.

money in his pockets, although officially, the cops recorded $7.70 on the dead body. It seems, in the end, the robber was robbed of his life, his brain, and his money.

But thanks to him and other cutthroat gangsters, law enforcement got a boost. Local police forces upgraded their cars, weapons, and training in order to combat future lawbreakers. Cops put two-way radios in their faster, bulletproof squad cars and wore bulletproof vests, just like the bad guys. Highly trained and heavily armed SWAT teams were created to deal with men like Dillinger. Soon, police were outwitting bad guys all over the place, and the gangster era came to a close by the 1940s and World War II.

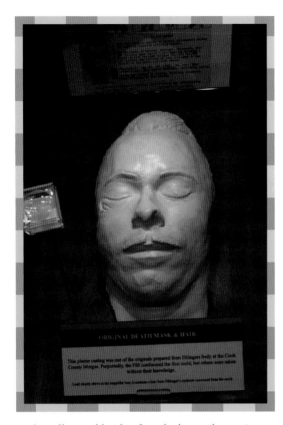

ORIGINAL DEATH MASK & HAIR

This plaster casting was one of the originals prepared from Dillinger's body at the Cook County Morgue. Purportedly, the FBI confiscated the first mold, but others were taken without their knowledge.

A really terrible idea for a bedroom decoration.

Banks also learned from Dillinger. They invested in better security, including armed guards and higher railings to prevent other long-legged criminals from jumping into their vaults. They also installed twenty-four-hour security systems. In the coming years, prisons were made more like fortresses with barbed wire and machine gun towers to prevent prisoner escapes. That's not to mention the power J. Edgar Hoover would wield for decades to come. He tacked the word Federal onto his Bureau of Investigation, and the blossoming crime fighting force got a new name. The name change was officially signed into law on March 22, 1935, less than a year after Dillinger's death.

Today, the FBI shoots higher than stolen cars and Old Faithful. More than 35,000 employees protect America from terrorism, cyber-attacks, and big-time criminals on US soil. It's one of the largest and most effective law enforcement agencies in the world.

Sometimes it only takes one really rotten egg to get people's attention and make change happen.

Lived: Nineteenth to twentieth centuries CE, England
Occupation: Suffragette

Emmeline Pankhurst

"No" Is Not in Her Dictionary

Damsels in Distress Need Not Apply

Acting ladylike can be pretty suffocating. Between wearing the perfect outfit on every occasion and knowing all the proper etiquette, being a lady is exhausting. Take that to the pinky-extended extreme in **Victorian** times. Little ladies were expected to be made of sugar and spice and sit nicely in corsets. But like today, not every girl wanted to play tea party or spend all day up to her elbows in soapy water. To these ladies, being "ladylike" didn't mean pretending not to exist.

> **Victorian:**
> Nineteenth-century Britain is named after prim and proper Queen Victoria, and it is usually remembered for being stuffier than a teddy bear.

Emmeline Pankhurst was one of those little girls. She didn't plan on spending her life cleaning up after boys or staying inside the house knitting socks while the men had all the fun. When she grew up, she decided to do something radical. Emmeline ruffled all the feathers on those dowdy Victorian hats and irritated people more than itchy poison ivy, but in the end, her crazy tactics transformed the world.

Striking Hard

Emmeline couldn't help being political. Growing up in Manchester, England, meant political disagreement came with her morning crumpets. Her family was more of the "protest and yell a lot" type, rather than the "stiff upper lip" type most Brits favored. When Emmeline was twenty-one, she married a forty-year-old lawyer named Richard Pankhurst who also loved a good political cause. Their idea of date night included marching in picket lines and protesting various wrongs in the world. If he ever brought her chocolates, she'd probably distribute them to the poor.

The most tedious tea party ever.

Richard wasn't much to look at, but Emmeline was more interested in his high values. He believed in women's rights, education for the poor, and a bunch of other unpopular stuff at the time. The Pankhursts wouldn't be accepting an invitation for dinner from the Queen anytime soon, but they were okay with that.

union:

Workers banding together to protect their rights and to bargain as a group for better pay and working conditions.

Richard encouraged Emmeline to support causes important to her. So, instead of popping out babies and pushing around a mop, she helped form a **union** for women match makers. (These match makers didn't roam the streets with an arrow nocked in Cupid's bow. They dipped wood into the dangerous chemical phosphorous to create matches you can light on fire.)

Besides low wages, bad hours, and awful working conditions, women at these match-making factories were starting to get horrible diseases from the chemicals, like "phossy jaw," which rotted their lower face away to nothing. No one seemed to care about this, except Emmeline.

Emmeline helped raise enough money to tell those men in charge of the factory to either dip the matches themselves or to make some changes.

In the meantime, Emmeline joined a few other politically minded committees to keep things interesting. Working as a **Poor Law Guardian** meant she spent her days at workhouses for the poor. Emmeline saw how hard the poor had it, and it was more appalling than a day without tea. She spent her mornings feeding thousands of poor people, and she spent her nights observing seven- and eight-year-old girls scrubbing the cold stone floors of the workhouse in threadbare dresses so they could get a piece of toast to eat.

Poor Law Guardian:

People who were responsible for helping the poor.

Obviously, this did not sit well with Emmeline. She demanded change, and within six months, she got it. The poor living in the workhouse got better food (bread with margarine on it), better clothes, and school instead of manual labor for the kids.

Amid all that protesting, Emmeline also found time to push out a few babies—five in total. Only her three girls made it to adulthood, though, and Richard didn't last long, either. When he died, Emmeline was devastated. Richard had been her partner in crime. He understood her completely. Now she'd have to stand up for the downtrodden on her own. She might even have to break the law, but she was okay with that. As a woman, she hadn't gotten to vote on what became a law in the first place, so why should she care if she broke it?

Sisters before Misters

To make ends meet after Richard died, Emmeline left the Poor Law Guardians and found work at the Registrar of Births and Deaths, writing down birth and death dates. It wasn't fancy, but it paid the bills. It also sparked more fury in the feisty lady.

Everywhere she turned, women got no respect, especially poor women. They didn't get to make the laws, but if they broke them, they were arrested by men, tried by men, and sentenced by men. Even no-brainers like going to law school was off-limits to girls. If things were going to change, women needed to be able to vote and help make the rules; otherwise, they'd always be treated as second-class citizens. That realization put a new cause in Emmeline's heart—the right to vote for women.

Parliament:

Like Congress in America, British Parliament has the sole power to make laws. It is led by the Prime Minister.

First, Emmeline tried the ladylike approach. She asked members of **Parliament** to support women's suffrage—a woman's right to vote in political elections.

For a few years, she made speeches asking for help, but men really weren't listening. When they did hear her, it led to a lot of empty promises or outright rudeness. Maybe talk wasn't enough.

Emmeline wanted "deeds not words." When a branch of the political party she and Richard had joined banned women, it was the straw that broke the **feminist's** back. Emmeline quit the party and made her own—no boys allowed. The Women's Social and Political Union (WSPU) was born, and Emmeline liked the idea of "deeds not words" so much that she made it the WSPU's motto and followed it loyally. Her fellow members were called suffragettes, which just means women protesting for the right to vote. It didn't matter what type of background a woman came from—any woman could join the cause. It was sisters before misters, and gender was way more important than money or skin color.

feminist:

A person who thinks women should have the same rights and opportunities as men.

Next, the WSPU pulled together a uniform of green, purple, and white. With that fashion crisis out of the way, Emmeline focused on her *pièce de résistance*—actual deeds. Deeds like standing on chairs and shouting questions at men while holding banners that read: VOTES FOR WOMEN. The horror!

Fashion crisis averted!

To the men in the room, it did seem horrible, and police manhandled Emmeline and the WSPU members to the nearest jail cell. The suffragettes could talk till they ran out of air, but it did diddly squat. Ladies weren't being listened to, and they weren't getting the vote, so maybe it was time to stop acting like ladies.

"I Am What You Call a Hooligan"

Emmeline knew the suffragettes had to step up their game in a big way. Emmeline did what she had to do, encouraging women to fight back with violence if necessary. She never condoned violence against people, just property,

Fake hair really adds something, don't you think?

but it still shocked the pompous British to their snooty core to see women throwing bricks at shop windows and generally making mayhem.

Emmeline's militancy even inspired Gandhi, who wrote about the suffragettes and started his own campaign to win Indian freedom from the British. At this point, the British might have been wondering, why us? But regular people were tired of being told what to do by pasty white men in fake wigs.

Soon, Emmeline was traveling the country, rousing up the rabble and generally being as big a nuisance as possible. Her supporters broke windows with their stone throwing, poured acid on golf courses (if men had nothing fun to do, maybe they'd start listening!), smashed mail boxes, defaced the walls inside Parliament, chained themselves to gates, and burned empty government buildings. Even when they threw stones because the prime minister refused to see them, the women took care to wrap them as nice little presents tied with a string. That way they wouldn't hurt anyone who happened to be looking outside at the time.

Nothing can hold me!

Police officers became exhausted trying to deal with these rowdy women in big purple dresses and frilly hats. Once a suffragette was arrested, she'd go on a hunger strike in jail. One suffragette refused to eat dinner, declaring she'd feast on her "determination" instead. That left the police with a big problem, which was exactly the point. Starving women in prison attracted way too much negative attention, so the government approved force-feeding them, which was a nasty business.

If a woman refused to eat while in jail, a steel jaw opener pushed her gums apart and held her mouth open while a doctor forced a rubber tube down her throat. Then the doctor forced liquefied food into her stomach. One woman recorded being force-fed 139 times during a three-month sentence for the suffragette cause.

Emmeline didn't let her girls have all the fun. She got in on the action, too. After she was arrested for conspiracy to destroy property (who needs golf courses, anyway?), a hunger strike in jail seemed appropriate.

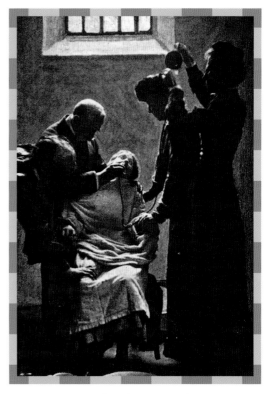

No fine dining in jail.

When doctors came to force-feed her, Emmeline held a clay jug over her head and threatened to brain anyone who got too close. They left her alone after that.

Eventually, authorities realized this was a no-win situation. They had to do something to stop all the hunger strikes. Authorities knew they couldn't let women starve to death in prison for throwing rocks—rock throwing marked a good protest. The government's force-feeding program was getting a lot of negative press, too, so some genius came up with the Cat and Mouse Act of 1913.

This act allowed hunger-striking suffragettes to refuse food all they wanted until they were weaker than a newborn pinky (a baby mouse). Once the mice were practically falling over with hunger, the government cats released the women home to recuperate and only re-arrested them after they regained their strength. The government hoped to toy with the mice until they gave in and admitted defeat.

Except Emmeline wasn't a typical frightened mouse. She had a plan. She figured the police could only re-arrest her if they caught her.

Mice with Tiger Teeth

Emmeline couldn't waste time hiding from police. She had rallies to throw, people to rouse, and speeches to make. She was an important public figure who traveled beyond Britain's borders to America and Canada with her message of equal rights for women. In order to keep herself from getting caught by police during her speeches, Emmeline recruited her very own bodyguards, which she named the Bodyguard. Short, sweet, and to the point.

The Bodyguard was a highly trained female fighting machine. Taught and led by women, the Bodyguard surrounded and protected Emmeline from the police during her public appearances, giving her enough time to escape. Her Bodyguard armed themselves with wooden clubs, flower pots, umbrellas, and hammers, and they were more than happy to fight their way out of any situation. Some police admitted fighting the Bodyguard girls was the toughest fight they'd ever been in.

In scuffles with the police, nobody played nice. Emmeline's women used Japanese self-defense tactics called *jujitsu* to scare the living daylights out of men by flipping them over their dainty shoulders. Police took a more frontal approach and punched, kicked, and assaulted the women, even giving them purple nurples. Why? Because not only did nipple pinching hurt, but it also— the police believed—gave the women breast cancer. Prince Charmings they were not.

Fight Like a Girl!

Trailblazing isn't easy. Luckily for Edith Garrud, she knew how to kick some serious butt, which happened to be her line of work anyway. After studying jujitsu during a time when women kept their ankles covered in public, Edith became one of the first female martial arts instructors in the Western world, even starting a school for jujitsu with her husband. It didn't take long for people to notice how awesome she was at this fighting thing, and they cast her as the lead in a silent action film. For publicity, a six-foot-tall police officer agreed to "test" her. As if Edith needed testing. At a fun-sized four-foot ten-inches tall, Edith took about 2.3 seconds to whip the man over her head and smash him to the ground. It's no wonder Emmeline tapped her as the Bodyguard's teacher. Edith trained thirty women in her dojo (her training school), whose main purpose was to beat up police officers and help Emmeline escape re-arrest.

THE SUFFRAGETTE THAT KNEW JIU-JITSU.
The Arrest.

Come and get me!

The Bodyguard couldn't always overcome an entire police force, and Emmeline was re-arrested twelve times in 1912 alone. But when they did go Karate Kid and beat the police at their own game, it really embarrassed the men. Emmeline would escape and laugh all the way to her next speaking engagement.

On a few occasions, Emmeline used cunning as well as a good ol' one-two to the nose to escape. She also used decoys to slip home without detection. The cats were furious.

Emmeline and the suffragettes entered a vicious cycle of violence, assaults, arrests, hunger strikes, and hiding from the police only to taunt them at the next meeting. After her tenth hunger strike, Emmeline's fifty-six-year-old intestinal tract wasn't getting any younger. Her health took a steady nose-dive, but there was no backing down now. It'd been decades of fighting, and Emmeline was ready to give her life for this important cause. The only thing that would stop her and the Bodyguard was getting the vote.

Or the Germans.

Flip-Flopper

In 1914, at the height of Emmeline's struggle with British police, Germany changed the game. War has an odd way of bringing people together, and World War I was no exception. Rightly or wrongly, Emmeline decided there would be no votes for *anyone* if Germany, Britain's foe, won the war, because there would be no Britain.

She called a truce with the battered British police and changed "Votes for Women" to "Support Britain." Then she urged all women to take up the cause and show men they deserved the vote. Most suffragettes rallied behind their leader and picked up the slack on jobs men left behind when they went to the trenches. Other women didn't want war at all, and still others didn't like the idea of supporting a government that wouldn't let them decide if they should go to war or not. Many women felt betrayed by Emmeline.

But Emmeline wasn't exactly democratic. It was her way or the highway. (Which, yes, is sort of the opposite of what she wanted men to do—be more democratic.) She exiled one of her own daughters to Australia when she didn't toe the WSPU line, and Emmeline publicly made fun of her other daughter when the young woman said Britain should stay out of the war.

Hi-Ya!

As for the British men, they suddenly started seeing Emmeline in a new light; one that would help their cause. They agreed to a truce, and all mice were released from prison. Emmeline kept doing what she was good at—speech-making—but now she rallied women to help the war effort and persuaded men to enlist. The new poster child for patriotism was even sent to Russia by the Prime Minister to persuade the Russians to stay in the war and continue fighting Germany. Yes, times had changed.

By 1918, Germany had surrendered, but Emmeline hadn't. Like a bloodhound with a scent, she pushed for women's rights again. Didn't women practically win the war by helping at home? Wasn't it time to treat them as equal citizens?

It seemed the government finally agreed (or they really dreaded the thought of more *jujitsuing* women). Women over thirty who owned property were given the right to vote after fifty long years of asking for it. Victory! Sort of. It took another ten years before all people over twenty-one, regardless of gender or property, got the right to vote.

Emmeline's violent methods were as polarizing as Brussels sprouts. You either loved her or hated her, but in the end, she helped get things done. Unfortunately for her, Emmeline died one month before universal suffrage was passed in **Britain**.

Britain:

In 1918, women over thirty were given the right to vote, but it wasn't until 1928 that women and men were given equal voting rights. American women got the right to vote with the passage of the Nineteenth Amendment in 1920, although some states gave women equal rights as early as 1869 (Go Wyoming!).

Two years later, thousands gathered to watch a statue of her unveiled to much trumpeting and fanfare. Suddenly, everyone thought she was cool again.

Lived: Twentieth century CE, America and Europe

Occupation: Special Operations Officer

Chapter 11

Virginia Hall

Limping Wins the Race

Better Than James Bond

Someone nicknamed "the Woman with the Limp" doesn't sound like the most dangerous spy during World War II, but don't say that to the Nazis. To them, Virginia Hall, a.k.a. the Limping Lady, was scarier than jumping out of an airplane without a parachute. A **Gestapo** reward poster had a sketch of Virginia and a memo running through the office that said: "She is the most dangerous of all Allied spies. We must find and destroy her." So they really weren't kidding.

In a world riddled with sabotage, a spy had to be pretty impressive to get that level of attention. Virginia Hall was that impressive. She didn't let little things like having one leg or a blown cover stop her from helping the Allies win World War II. As one of the earliest secret

Gestapo:

The secret police of the Nazi party. The Gestapo were brutal and ruthless in their methods for finding "enemies of the state." But they never could find Virginia.

agents in the war, both men and women looked up to her. It's not hard to see why. Virginia saved countless agents, organized Nazi resistance, killed 150 German soldiers, and managed to capture an additional 500 of them throughout the course of the war. And *then* she paved the way for women CIA agents. Beat that, James Bond.

How Not to Drop a Gun

Virginia Hall was born in 1906, and lucky for her, it was to a wealthy family, but she didn't want money for the same reasons that others wanted money. Instead of buying fancy dresses or hosting fabulous balls, Virginia wanted to learn languages and study abroad. In fact, while most of Virginia's friends were plotting how to hook a man, she was plotting how to hook a career. She wanted to be a diplomat, preferably in Europe, because America was pretty boring in her eyes.

So she made it happen and bounced around Europe for a while, stockpiling languages like canned goods. Virginia learned French, Italian, and German, but not how to be gutsy—she was born knowing that.

Because of her language know-how, Virginia landed jobs working in US embassies in exotic places like Estonia, Austria, and Poland. While stationed in Turkey, she negotiated more than peace. On a bird hunting trip, she shot herself right in the foot. She dropped her gun and caught it by the trigger, which everyone knows is the wrong way to catch a gun. Doctors amputated her leg below the **knee**.

knee:

Virginia nicknamed her new prosthetic leg Cuthbert. Cuthbert was wooden with a rubber sole, covered in horse hide, and weighed a hefty seven pounds. Virginia then proceeded to learn how to walk again with all that extra baggage. No wonder she limped.

As if having one leg wasn't bad enough, the US State Department in charge of hiring foreign service officers said Virginia couldn't join their office anymore. They had a strict no amputee policy. Whatever; it was their loss. Virginia resigned, rather than be chained to a desk, and skipped over to Paris a bit heavier thanks to Cuthbert.

Pedal to the Metal

Maybe it was the danger. Maybe it was the adventure. Maybe it was because Virginia was an adrenaline junkie before swimming with sharks was acceptable. Whatever it was, when Nazi Germany invaded Poland in September 1939 and started World War II, Virginia and Cuthbert didn't flee Paris like most normal people. Not one to sit around like she only had one leg or something, Virginia signed on to be an ambulance driver as soon as Hitler turned his eyes toward Paris.

Driving an ambulance with one leg in the middle of a war was a lot scarier than swimming with sharks. It was kind of like riding a roller coaster without a seatbelt. Virginia took a four-week training class to learn basic medical treatments for the wounded as well as how to defend herself. Then she had to figure out how to drive a car with only one real foot. Since all cars were manual in the 1940s, Virginia had to use her wooden foot for the clutch and her right foot for the gas for hours on end.

It wasn't glamorous. Virginia bumped around on a hard wooden bench all day, her sweaty stump chafing against the wooden leg while she listened to men die in the back of her truck. Personal hygiene wasn't really a thing either;

Putting the rubber to the metal.

when she got to splash a bucket of water over her head, Virginia considered it a good day. Forget about laundry or a feather mattress. She made do with blood-encrusted shirts and straw as a bed. Despite being in France, the food was far from fancy. Spam and powdered eggs became five-star delicacies.

Then the worst happened. France surrendered, and Virginia had to flee to Britain to avoid living in a hostile, occupied country. Because she loved France so much, she wanted to serve up a dish of cold revenge to whatever Nazis was dumb enough to tangle with her.

Her own country, the United States, rejected her based on her two "handicaps" (being a woman and having one leg), so Virginia joined the British **SOE** to keep fighting the Nazis. Before she could smash Nazis, she had to go through an intensive training program.

SOE:

Special Operations Executives—British spies with only one mission: take down Hitler.

For the next three weeks, seven days a week, Virginia and eleven other women made Rambo look like Bambi. They shot, stabbed, ran, and broke men's jaws in hand-to-hand combat. They memorized long messages, secretly disposed of paper trails, operated field radios, learned Morse code, and, most important of all, mastered the art of lying. They had to be ruthless and tidy in their lies. In the field, they would be expected to do months of lying, all in a different language. Having friends or boyfriends was out of the question, since it could get them killed.

Only four women made it through, and Virginia was one of them.

Then came phase two of training. The final four weeks required more guns, knives, and fighting, but it also included side acts of map reading, night raiding, plane jumping, and blowing fake railroads to smithereens. No one gave the ladies a break because they were women. There's no crying in spying, even if it's on a cross-country hike and one of the women only has one leg.

The last SOE test involved being pulled from bed in the middle of the night, screamed at in German about being a spy, and getting ice cold water thrown on them to make them confess. Virginia passed, obviously, and became one of the first women field agents in the SOE.

Vichy France:
The part of France not directly under German military supervision after France fell.

Finally, Virginia was ready for her cover story, code name, and cover name. She would be known as a French-speaking reporter working for the *New York Post* in **Vichy France**, code name Germaine to the SOE. To the public, her cover name was Brigitte LeContre.

Tiresome Cuthbert

Virginia was given a million francs to stuff in a waistband and put on the train to Vichy. Sure, she could have hightailed it home, a million francs richer, but betrayal wasn't her style. Another train took her to the city of Lyon in Vichy France. Here, Virginia thwarted the Germans so many times, they began circulating posters about the Lady with a Limp.

Despite being a fugitive, Virginia still found time to do annoying things like recruit men and women to help the Resistance (against Germany), sabotage German vehicles, supply other SOE agents with money and papers, and help downed pilots get to safety. She juggled multiple code names, allies, and enemies all while eluding German agents and writing articles for the *Post* to keep up her cover. James Bond couldn't hold a lipstick-smeared martini glass to her.

For a few of the male pilots, being told to trust a woman with their lives after parachuting into hostile territory seemed a bit like trusting a toddler to preform brain surgery. But it was either that or go it alone. They all chose Virginia. Soon, she was known as the go-to woman for any fly boy shot down in the area.

Virginia had been in the field for fifteen months. Most agents got six months at a time—if they made it that long. The average life expectancy of a radio operator was six weeks. She hadn't been caught yet, but word on the street was the Germans were invading the rest of France, and they wanted to find and fry her. Slowly.

Virginia had no intention of frying after a perfect record of not being caught, so she fled while she still could. Along with a guide and three other Resistance fighters, Virginia scuttled over the Pyrenees Mountains in November of 1942. The group needed to escape France, enter Spain secretly, take a few trains, and then hop a boat to England. Piece of cake. Except for the part where it was all illegal, not to mention dangerous, and the fact that her likeness was all over reward posters searching for the Limping Lady.

Virginia was the only woman and the only one packing a wooden leg for the journey, but that didn't mean she wanted special treatment. In fact, she kept the no-leg part a secret, because her mountain guide was already grumbling about having to take a woman. Despite the snow drifts being higher than her knees, wearing wet socks that caused her stump to blister everywhere, and having to snowplow with her real leg and drag the fake one behind her, Virginia kept up with the men. The only time she came close to complaining was when she signaled London from a rest house in the mountains that Cuthbert was being unruly.

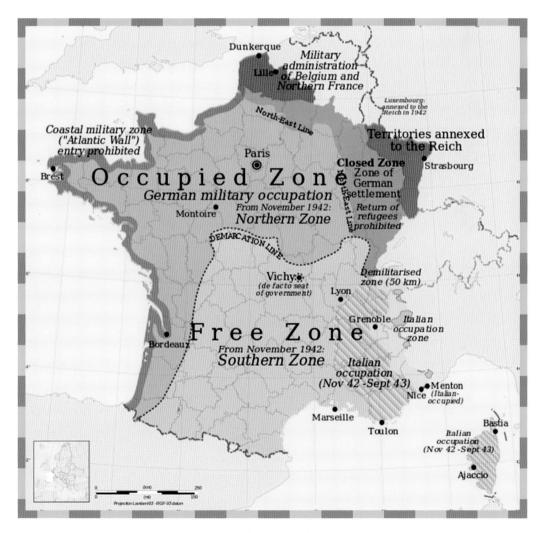

Vichy, France—in purple—was a dangerous place to live.

London let Virginia know she could "eliminate" Cuthbert if necessary. They thought her pet name for her leg was one of the men. Now she really was as cool as James Bond. She had a license to kill.

It should have been smooth sailing once she got over the mountains and down the other side into Spain.

Of course it wasn't that easy.

Raring to Go

Sometimes the early bird doesn't catch the worm. Sometimes the early bird *is* the worm. When Virginia and the three Frenchmen met at 4:30 a.m. to catch the 5:45 train out of town, all they wanted was to avoid Spanish guards who might ask too many questions. Unfortunately, the guards weren't feeling lazy that morning. They had some spunk in their step and were at the train station checking passports. Without proper stamps, the four fugitives were carted off to a Spanish jail.

Luckily for Virginia, the Spanish and Germans didn't compare notes. Like Girl Scouts peddling cookies, the Gestapo were still going door-to-door with posters of the Limping Lady in France, all while she was cooling her blistered stump in a Spanish jail cell. Virginia didn't twiddle her thumbs and reminisce about how awesome a spy she was while locked up; she made friends with her cellmate. When her cellmate was sprung a few weeks later, she smuggled a letter straight to the American embassy. The Americans pulled some strings, got Virginia out, and the SOE's female agent was in London by Christmas. The Nazis never knew how close they'd come to capturing their nemesis.

It only took a few months of sitting around in London, not beating up on Nazis, before Virginia was itching to get back in the game. She was assigned to Madrid, Spain, which wasn't exactly what she wanted, but at least she was spying again. This time, she posed as a journalist for the *Chicago Times*. But her previous adventures in Lyon, the mountains, and jail made Virginia feel like she was losing her brain cells to boredom in Spain.

For some reason, every time she mentioned getting back to Nazi-occupied France, her superiors shot her down. It was like the SOE thought she was crazier than a rabid raccoon for wanting to get back to where the action was. They knew Virginia would be risking her neck (and everyone else's) if she got caught, and the Nazi's were on to the queenpin with a limp.

To show the SOE how very serious she was, Virginia turned down a public ceremony for an award presented by the king of Britain himself. He wasn't *her* king, and spies needed to keep a low profile. Then she heard about the American version of SOE, the **OSS**.

OSS:

Office of Strategic Services—American spies led by William "Wild Bill" Donovan, which should give you some idea as to the way things were run.

Apparently, the OSS accepted crazies in their ranks. Every type of person from circus performers to former thieves to Julia Child (future famous cook) was welcomed. That didn't mean they were hopelessly incompetent. The OSS was also responsible for little jewels of sabotage like the infamous Exploding Camel Dung trick practiced in the deserts of Morocco. Nazi tanks didn't stand a chance rolling over those innocent looking piles of poo.

Worse than flaming bags of poo left on doorsteps.

Virginia wanted in, so she quickly got herself transferred. Once accepted into the OSS, she bee-lined straight for France, using her skills on the wireless radio and Morse code to play spy at night and milkmaid by day. Changing her cover to a more low-key job wouldn't solve the problem of that limp, however, so Virginia fixed that.

First, she died her brown hair gray and threw a headscarf over it. Then, she bulked up her physique to a decidedly more matronly look. She didn't become a gym rat or down protein drinks; instead, she bought puffy skirts and stuffed as many layers under her jacket as a royal wedding cake. Finally, she practiced a shuffling gait to disguise her limp and to match her new, crazy cat lady look. Virginia, code-named Diane, was back to teach the Nazis a lesson.

She used her makeover to roam the French countryside as a milkmaid and goat herder, gathering D-Day intelligence on German troop positions, drop sites, and possible safe-houses. She was constantly on the move, and all the info she gathered was communicated back to England via a radio transmitter that she carried in her suitcase. Virginia didn't just work harder, she also worked smarter.

One of Virginia's many identification cards.

She recruited again, and within six months, she had three hundred operational agents working with her—her own little army to rival Hitler's.

Virginia's team, code-named HECKLER, helped with pre-D-Day sabotage. One step behind the Germans, they removed German explosives on bridges the Allies would need after they arrived. They also attacked anything the Nazis might need—things like trains, roads, phone stations, and local headquarters. This time, the Nazis had no idea they were up against the Limping Lady. Had they known, they may have thrown in the *Handtuch* then and there.

A Cheesy Ending

Virginia had one more trick up her frumpy dress sleeve while in Vichy France. Besides roaming the countryside looking innocent and trying to keep a low profile, she also made and sold goat cheese directly to the Nazis. It was risky, but secretly knowing German allowed her to eavesdrop—as long as she kept up the ancient French woman act. When she retired at the mandatory age of sixty with her husband, fellow OSS agent Paul Goillot, she used all that cheese-making knowledge to produce the best goat cheese this side of the Atlantic.

Virginia spent her days bicycling up and down mountains with Cuthbert, and her nights waiting for parachute drops with supplies for her band of resistors. She was the first to report when the Nazis moved headquarters to a new town. Although no one let her participate directly in the sabotage she coordinated, her plans battered and demoralized the German army. She was much too important to risk capture, and the Gestapo were still trying to "find and destroy" the Limping Lady.

Soon, the Nazis had more important things to worry about, like retreating from the victorious Allies. The war was coming to an end. Virginia had come through it hunted but never found.

A Virginia Hall–Sized Job

Virginia had done well. For all that hard work, she became the first woman awarded the Distinguished Service Cross for extreme valor, and President Truman decided to award it personally. That is, until Virginia turned him down, just like she did the king of England. She wanted to continue spying and that meant *secrecy*. Why didn't anyone get that?

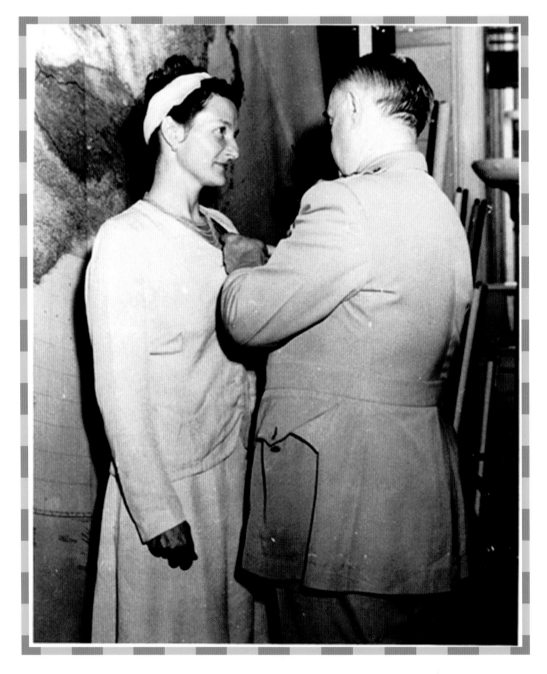

Virginia received her award in private from Wild Bill Donovan.

What Virginia wanted, she usually got, and this time, she wanted to be the first woman on the CIA's staff. Except she was given a desk job. Sitting around planning other spies' dangerous missions would never suit her, but the new bosses—young men who scoffed at old, one-legged women—didn't think Virginia could carry out anything, including her own plans. Like muskets and slingshots today, she was obsolete.

Although Virginia had risked capture, torture, and death to stop Hitler, she never got back into the field. Instead, she paved the way for women to be more than secretaries— they could become full-blown CIA spies. As the first woman on the CIA's Career Staff, Virginia sat at her desk and helped prep war plans in case America ever went back to war.

Someone once told Virginia's mother that Virginia was

Cooler than Charlie's Angels

Despite the threat of torture, dismemberment, and death, lots of women rushed to fill the role of spy in the OSS under the leadership of Wild Bill.

For more information on women in World War II, find links and other information at:

www.briannadumont.com/resources

Ladies, if you think you've got what it takes to work for the CIA, know that five out of the top eight officers are women and that 40 percent of the agency's undercover spies are women. It was also a "sisterhood" of CIA women who tracked down Osama Bin Laden. So start thinking about going to college (a degree is required) and boning up on a new language if you think spying might be your thing.

doing "a spectacular, man-sized job. . . .You have every reason to be proud of her." Perhaps what they should tell mothers of spies instead is that they are doing a spectacular, Virginia Hall–sized job.

Lived: Twentieth to twenty-first century CE, South Africa
Occupation: Lawyer, Activist, Revolutionary, Politician, President

Nelson Mandela

Jailbird

Rolihlahla Rolls off the Tongue

If your mom names you "troublemaker," she might be asking for it. In the case of Rolihlahla, a.k.a. **Nelson Mandela**, it was simply accurate. He was a major pain in the butt from day one, but it was a good thing. Life in South Africa needed shaking up, and Nelson was just the troublemaker to do it.

Nelson Mandela:

A white teacher christened him Nelson when she couldn't pronounce Rolihlahla because that was the thing to do in those days.

In a time when native Africans couldn't vote, own land, live where they wanted, speak freely, or even use the same sidewalks and elevators as whites, Nelson dared to say something. When he said it too loudly, he had to go on the run. It was either that or get thrown in jail (which happened, too).

Mandela went from living in a **cow dung** and mud-smeared hut to being elected South Africa's president in their first free election ever, which ended apartheid in South Africa. In the history of the world, it's hard to find someone more admired than him. Sure Mandela was a hero, a freedom fighter, Nobel Peace Prize winner, and so on, but he was also a big, fat criminal. In a good way.

cow dung:
Otherwise known as cow pie, cow chips, cow pats, or cow poop.

Mandela went on the run for the first time because he was pretty sure girls had cooties. Just kidding about the cooties, but it *was* because of a girl.

Fake It 'Til You Make It

When Nelson was nine, he went to live with a local ruling regent and his family. It was great; Nelson could watch how to govern properly, get

Qunu today, where twelve-year-old Nelson Mandela went to live. Electricity wasn't a thing in the village then.

a good education, and have **responsibilities**. Then the regent ruined it all by exercising his matchmaking muscles for both Nelson and his own son, Justice.

The boys decided they weren't going down the aisle without a fight, so they waited until the regent went on a trip. They stole a couple of his oxen, pawned them for some travel money, and got the heck out of there, wife-free.

Justice's dad wasn't regent for nothing, however. He remembered how scheming the two were together and told all the train stations to watch out for two runaways on their way to **Johannesburg**. Just a hunch.

A furious train conductor confronted the doomed boys. But Nelson was a sweet talker and always had been. He pointed out that they really hadn't broken any laws (oxen aside), so he couldn't keep them against their will. The train conductor gave up in the face of

responsibilities:

Mandela's favorite was ironing shirts. Seriously. Probably because he arrived at the regent's palace wearing a pair of his dad's pants cut to fit him and tied with a string. Nelson learned one should dress snazzy to be snazzy.

Johannesburg:

The economic capital and most populated city in South Africa. Johannesburg was where dreams were made and broken in the shadows of electric lights.

The Power of Green Jell-O
(Otherwise Known as Revolting Cafeteria Offerings)

Actually, it wasn't just the cooties that made young Nelson run away from the regent. It was a combination of his arranged marriage and getting kicked out of college due to his first stand against the establishment. Nelson had recently been elected to a student council–type board at school, which was great. Not so great was the food at lunch and the fact that the all-white faculty had way more power than the all-black students. As a result, most students boycotted the election and refused to vote with a rallying cry of "Better food, more power! Better food, more power!" When the teachers didn't listen, Nelson quit the council and refused to be on it without open elections. The principal didn't appreciate Nelson's morals and expelled him until he agreed to serve on the council. Nelson never agreed. Between no school and an arranged marriage looming over his head, he decided to try his luck in the big city.

Time to make the world a better place.

all that logic, and the boys were free again. It was good training for what Nelson really wanted to do—practice law.

The regent tried tracking down the boys for a while. He finally gave up on Nelson, but not on Justice. That kid was supposed to be the future chief. As for Nelson, he could mess up his life however he wanted to. There were no chiefdoms in his destiny. Despite laws making it tougher for Africans to get into law school than actually surviving law school, Nelson was determined to make that his destiny.

After Justice went home, Nelson found a paying job in a law office. His salary didn't cover all the basics like food, housing, and tuition, but Nelson coped. His first apartment didn't have electricity, running water, or a proper floor. Sometimes he didn't eat, and he had to walk nine miles to and from work to save enough money to buy candles for light to do his homework. But hey! He was making it in the big city. Sure, a dead body popped up every once in a while outside his apartment and no one did anything about it, but it wasn't his body.

After Nelson received his bachelor's degree, his boss gave him a raise (which he used for more candles), and he got into one of only four universities that allowed blacks to take law classes. Then Nelson started to get political. He joined the ANC—the African National Congress—a group dedicated to waking up African political activity, since, despite being native to the land and in the majority, they had no power. A bunch of white men were in charge.

Indians:

Natives from India were typically merchants and richer than the native African farmers. This made everyone, including whites, jealous.

Gandhi:

An Indian lawyer who lived in South Africa for twenty-one years. He later encouraged peaceful resistance to attain self-rule in India.

Nelson didn't yet have what you'd call "blind tolerance" so much as "blind hatred" for both whites and **Indians** living in South Africa. The tolerance thing would come later. Peaceful resistance was all fine and good for people like **Gandhi**, but Nelson wanted to go nuclear. To him, only violence and Africans themselves could make things better, which doesn't exactly sound heroic. But to understand his early beliefs, you have to understand the laws he lived under: apartheid.

Apartheid Sucks

The white minority avoided the native Africans like Meatloaf Mondays. They were obsessed with separation. Apartheid literally means "apartness." Official laws took over South Africa in 1948, but separation was already the rule of the day. Making it official meant that everyone had to register what race they were so "the enforcement of any existing or future laws" could be done better.

A person's race was decided by appearance, reputation, and general acceptance—however the big guys in charge decided those things. Race determined everything from what schools you went to, and what jobs you were qualified for, to how much you got paid, and where you could live. Want to go to the beach or take the bus? Your race determined which ones you could use. The same was true for who you could date, which neighborhood you could live in, and where you could be buried after you died. Apartheid ruled every aspect of life (and death) in South Africa.

To make sure those in charge could control the flow of Africans to "white areas," the government passed laws putting a seventy-two-hour restriction on African visitors to what-ever places whites wanted for themselves. Limiting the amount of land Africans could live on meant almost a million people were left without homes. Later, more laws were passed separating housing for races "to elim-inate friction" because see-ing a person with different skin color "must be avoided." Even worse, Africans weren't allowed to vote or participate in government at all, so they had no input on these import-ant issues, which is what you call really messed up.

The ANC wasn't okay with that, but their meth-ods of peaceful resistance weren't working. They held a Defiance Campaign, where volunteers broke curfew and

Maybe the sand is different?

went to whites-only places. More than eight thou-sand people were **arrested** during the cam-paign, including Mandela, who got his first taste of prison for two days. The peaceful protest didn't change the government's mind, but it did change Mandela's.

About the only success that grew out of the Defiance Campaign was Mandela's real-ization that the fight against apartheid should be multiracial. He still thought violence was the

arrested:

Before the event, the organizers handed the police detailed lists stating the participants' names and addresses in order for the anticipated arrests to be more orderly.

Deciding who lives where . . . nary a native in sight.

way to make change happen, but at least it was progress. Encouraging his people to take up weapons and attack white policemen, though, didn't help his cause.

When the ANC made their next move, Mandela wasn't allowed near the meetings. He was officially banned by the government from political activity for two years thanks to his loud mouth and that violence talk. The ANC, along with a few other groups, decided to write up a Freedom Charter, which included a bunch of highfalutin ideas about equality, food, and land for everyone. They didn't provide a whole lot of practical suggestions, but it sounded nice. Mandela watched from the sidelines, disguised as a milkman to avoid the police. It was good practice for the future.

When the guys in charge heard about this so-called Freedom Charter, it freaked them out big time. Mandela and 155 others were arrested and charged with treason. Treason, of course, came with a noose attached.

Bouncing from Jail to Jail

Mandela spent the next four years on trial with the threat of death hanging over his head. He didn't have to stay in jail the whole time, so it was business as usual with his **law partner**. However, business was scarce. Being on trial himself sort of dried it up. Before, the firm was swamped with petty crimes thanks to petty apartheid laws. Now, Mandela's own trial consumed his energy. What cases the partners got often required hours of travel to courthouses in different cities. White judges made it as difficult as possible for them to do their job well. The judges changed the times of trials without notifying them, pretended clients had asked for another lawyer, and insisted Mandela didn't have the right credentials. Pretty soon, their law business went belly up.

law partner:

Mandela and his friend, Oliver Tambo, opened South Africa's first black law firm the same year as the Defiance Campaign began, although Mandela wouldn't technically receive his law degree until fifty years after he started studying— while in jail.

While the ANC and its leaders were on trial, other pro-African organizations tried to get the change ball rolling. When the Pan-Africanist Congress (PAC) organized a campaign in Sharpeville, five thousand Africans gathered to protest apartheid laws. Police got panicky and fired into the crowd, without stopping, until 67 people were killed and over 180 others were wounded. The losses were great and the PAC didn't change much. In fact, it was pretty much a dismal failure, just like the Defiance Campaign.

Then the government really freaked out. They declared a state of emergency, banned all organizations—including the ANC—and arrested whoever they could find . . . without getting warrants first. Mandela's kids watched as the police rifled through his stuff and carted him off to jail.

arrest:

Mandela was the only person named for organizing a strike, which was illegal, so he was the only one the government could arrest. Just the way he planned it. In the end, Mandela considered the strike a failure and called it off after one day. No one really understands why.

For hours, police refused to give the prisoners food or water or decent blankets, unless you consider lice and vomit fun bedmates. Finally, the rest of the world started to pay attention to the warped intentions of the South Africa government. Too bad the government didn't listen to the world asking them to stop.

Mandela stayed behind bars for five months, demanding better food and sleeping arrangements. His smooth talking worked again, because the cells were deloused and the food improved before his release. Then it was back to court for the whole treason business. At least he got some good news there. The accused were found not guilty.

When the treason trial ended, a not-dead Mandela knew what to do. First, he jumped for joy. Second, he hid. After he heard the "not guilty" sentence, Mandela went underground. He didn't even go home that night. There was already another warrant out for his **arrest**. Life as a political activist was going to be a lot harder as a fugitive, but that didn't make Mandela decide to take the easy way out. He wasn't a (heroic) criminal for nothing!

Catch Me If You Can

Black Pimpernel:

Not to be confused with pumpernickel bread. The press's nickname for Mandela was based off a wily fictional character named the Scarlet Pimpernel from the French Revolution who couldn't be caught, either.

The first item on Mandela's new agenda as a fugitive was to avoid capture. *Duh*. He had safe houses, secret meetings, stealthy communications, and disguises galore. From fake beards to fake chauffeurs' uniforms, Mandela one-upped the frustrated police at every turn. Road blocks, helicopter searchlights, and night raids meant nothing to the **Black Pimpernel**!

From the underground, Mandela decided that all of the peaceful protests and non-violent demonstrations were getting him and his followers nowhere. The government just hired secret police and moved in troops all over Johannesburg. The time had come to pull another tool from the toolbox: violent demonstrations with as little loss of life as possible.

Many remained unconvinced that violence was the best way to go (since no one had any experience in warfare, and it *was* violent), but before Mandela was convinced. He set up *Umkhonto we Sizwe*, which means the Spear of the Nation, or MK for short. Its purpose was exactly what it sounds like—to make war.

Cooped up indoors during the day, Mandela studied the history of uprisings around the world. Sometimes he'd throw in some poetry to keep things interesting. At night, the fugitive would pop into secret meetings and organize the militant MK. Every few weeks, he'd move on to the next safe house.

Soon, MK was ready to begin its next campaign: sabotage. This would be a bit more explosive than the Defiance Campaign. Literally. Mandela graduated from reading about war to conducting war. He learned how to mix up the perfect batch of bombs all ready for government buildings, railways, and phone lines. If that didn't work, his backup plan included guerilla warfare.

After the first successful bombings, Mandela snuck out of South Africa and went on a tour of the rest of Africa and London. If peaceful demonstrations, strikes, and explosions didn't work, he wanted to be able to lead his troops into battle, and he wanted to have the supplies to do it well. That meant learning how to shoot a gun and getting other countries to pony up. After six months abroad gaining support, Mandela came home locked and loaded.

Then he got sloppy.

See, Mandela really liked the way he looked in uniform. He liked it so much, he never changed and he never shaved his beard. It felt good to be recognized, which was a big problem when police were dying to catch him. First rule for fugitives: change your look and change it often.

After seventeen months in hiding, Mandela got picked up while driving back from a sabotage planning session. Luckily for him and the MK, he wasn't

I feel freer . . .

arrested by Sherlock Holmes. The police didn't find the loaded gun or the notebooks full of co-conspirators' names and places to target next. Instead, they arrested Mandela for leaving the country without a passport.

At his next trial, Mandela dressed to impress. Instead of his newest obsession with military khakis, he chose the traditional route—real traditional. He wore his native tribal costume made of leopard skin and beads to emphasize how he was an African being judged by all whites.

He pled not guilty to encouraging the strike and leaving the country without a passport (even though he did), because he had no representation among those who made those laws.

The judge didn't care for Mandela's fancy speech-making and sentenced him to five years in prison. Not terrible in the grand scheme of life, until his equally sloppy friends got themselves caught, too. They weren't so lucky. Police found the whole enchilada with this raid, including maps, papers, bombs, and names. Worse, they found Mandela's handwritten diary, and it wasn't gushing about which girls he thought were cute. It was more military minded, and it included his recent travel itinerary outside of the country. (But there were a few love letters from his second wife, Winnie, in there to spice it up.)

Practically a Dystopian Bestseller

With all these new charges, Mandela's five years of smashing rocks in prison could turn into a noose real quick. The ten accused men were considered

Mandela University

Welcome to Mandela University. You won't get an actual degree to frame for your mom, but you'll learn stuff.

Nelson turned a five-year prison stint into a twenty-seven-year stay, much of which was spent on Robben Island. It wasn't the Ritz. Mandela's head and feet touched both ends of his cell when he laid down, which meant he had just enough room for a sleeping mat and a plastic pee bucket. Wake-up alarms went off at 5:30 a.m. but no one could leave his tiny cell until 6:45 a.m. Mandela kept from going crazy by running in place and doing sit-ups. Then it was off to the quarry to pound big rocks into little rocks for hours. Any rule breaking meant solitary confinement with only rice water for food. (This also meant chatting with the voices in your head was totally normal.) Luckily, Mandela's will to succeed hadn't been broken yet. He talked the prison into allowing everyone to take university classes if they wished. He helped other students study. He encouraged his fellow prisoners and guards to educate themselves and to disagree with each other respectfully. He learned another language (Afrikaans, the tongue of the oppressor), got his law degree, and wrote his autobiography.

Over the next ten years, things slowly got better. Bank robbers and baby killers were still treated better than the political prisoners like Mandela, but he got his first pair of underwear since he was jailed, so that was exciting. Prisoners also received a letter and a visit from family members once a month instead of twice a year, although Mandela wasn't allowed to touch so much as a fingernail of his wife Winnie's hand for the first twenty-one years he was jailed. Work at the quarry became more tolerable and Mandela spent a lot of his day giving academic lectures. By the time he was sprung, Mandela had graduated to a little cottage of his own with a swimming pool and personal chef. Clearly, the time for holding these political prisoners was over.

violent saboteurs and that meant the death penalty lay in store for them, again. After another **epic speech** by Mandela and six months of trials, the conspirators got slapped with life sentences instead. Mandela wouldn't see freedom again for twenty-seven years.

The rest of his friends also had to flee the country or risk a rock-breaking

epic speech:

Mandela's four-hour speech had little nuggets of gold destined to make even the most hard-hearted criminal get goose bumps. He faced the judge and let him know he was prepared to die for equality. If need be. But he'd rather live for it, you know?

Mandela's cell was a not-so-great place to crash after a day of breaking rocks.

destiny. Some were offered a one-way ticket out of South Africa, which was a lot nicer than the offer the fifty men sentenced to death got.

Outside prison, things got worse before they got better. The government cracked down on newspapers, radio, and television. Reading the wrong paper could get you three years in the slammer. Arrest without warrants became the norm. Jailers locked people up and swallowed the key. Investigators allowed torture tactics for suspects. It sounds like a science fiction novel, but it was just the 1960s in South Africa.

The '70s and '80s weren't any better. Violence reigned supreme on both sides. Mandela didn't want innocent people to die, but he still thought violence was inevitable. It was a classic cowboy case of neither side wanting to take their finger off the trigger first.

In the 1980s, Mandela secretly began negotiating with the new president of South Africa for his release from prison as well as the unbanning of the ANC. The whole world was chanting "Free Mandela!" by this point and putting pressure on the South African government. More and more young people got involved in the protest against apartheid and helped the cause for equality.

Finally, on February 11, 1990, after ten thousand days in prison, Nelson Mandela walked out a free man. The work wasn't done yet; apartheid laws were still in place, and violence still killed innocent people. It would take a few more years of talks to end more than forty years of separate everything, but in April 1994, it happened. Mandela was elected the first black president of South Africa in the first fully democratic election ever held. At the age of seventy-five, Mandela cast his first vote, ever. Having the majority of people cast a vote for him, too, was icing on the cake. It was a victory for justice and for humanity.

Not everything was sunshine and rainbows after Mandela's election, but that's to be expected with the birth of any government. The important thing is that now, everyone can have a say in how to make South Africa thrive. Today, Nelson Mandela is still a potent symbol. He embodies the hunger in all of us to be free and equal.

Acknowledgments

Thank you to my agent, Carrie Pestritto, for always looking ahead and for finding Julie Matysik, the perfect editor for this series; to Bethany Straker for capturing my voice in pictures; to Dr. Seth A. Parry for providing me with chapters four and five of his dissertation; and to my ever-supportive friends and family who I know would have my back while on the run. My sister, Andrea DuMont, might be more excited for this book than me—thanks for carrying copies of *Famous Phonies* to grocery stores, just waiting to pounce on a curious gaze to tell them all about this series. Mom, Dad, and Devin, your pride shines through me.

And, of course, this book and I would be a mere shadow without the help and love of my husband, Tim. Here's to Baby Hammerly, due August 19: may she not come on our wedding anniversary.

Notes on Sources

Chapter One

Much of Spartacus's life, and especially his emotions, thoughts, and motivations, are lost to us. Barry Strauss, military history professor at Cornell University, wrote a great book on the military aspect, which I used in addition to the University of Chicago's *Encyclopedia Romana* for information all about those kooky Romans. Ancient sources are also tricky to trust, since the earliest writings on Spartacus are a generation after his death and written by the very elite he was fighting against. I used Brent D. Shaw's *Spartacus and the Slave Wars* to read those ancient documents and ancient thoughts on the fugitive slave. What we have today on the rebel Spartacus is more myth than reality.

Chapter Two

Cleopatra has fascinated people for centuries. Maybe that's why the potential sources for her are unnerving—it's like looking at Mount Everest. I stuck to scholarly source materials from Dr. Duane W. Roller and Dr. Diane E.

E. Kleiner, even though academics themselves rarely agree on what happened or why. (I've said it before: if you like arguing, go into academia.) I did give myself one indulgence with Cassius Dio, a Roman historian who wrote in Greek during the second and third centuries CE.

Chapter Three

Martin Luther perhaps changed history more than any of our other fugitives. He is a fascinating ex-monk with plenty of literature on him. Many sources are outdated and usually contradict each other. It seems hard to determine Luther's thoughts, as it is with many characters from history. I used biographies by Derek Wilson and Marty Martin, as well as Professor Brian Sandberg's history blog for information on European religious wars.

Chapter Four

Reading about Koxinga means you get to read all about pirates! Jonathan Clements's book, *Koxinga and the Fall of the Ming Dynasty*, went into most of the pirate's life. Tonio Alexander Andrade's book covered Koxinga in Formosa and added extra tidbits like the stone lions Koxinga forced his men to carry.

Chapter Five

Queen Mary spent more time on the run than she did ruling Scotland. She was Scotland's only queen and, thus, extremely interesting (and controversial) to historians and humans everywhere. I relied on many books to try to dig up the truth behind the many conspiracy accusations leveled against her. Linda Porter's *Tudors versus Stewarts* gave a more sympathetic take on Mary, while Roderick Graham's *The Life of Mary, Queen of Scots* didn't give as much leeway to the fugitive queen. It was interesting to read two different views of the same woman, and her chapter in this book should reflect both sides.

Chapter Six

The Pilgrims are at the core of American mythology. It can be hard to find the truth when such potent symbols are involved. I looked at traditional sites like Pilgrim Hall Museum and William Bradford's firsthand account via Project Gutenberg. Nick Bunker's book, *Making Haste from Babylon*, illuminated their years in England and as fugitives in Holland.

Chapter Seven

As a celebrity even in her lifetime, Harriet Tubman got a lot of publicity. Milton Sernett did a great job debunking the fantastical myths around Tubman. Montgomery's raid came from the University of North Florida's website and from Sarah Bradford's account (the somewhat fantastical Tubman biographer), which she heard straight from the horse's mouth.

Chapter Eight

Poor Mary Mallon. Forever will she be known as Typhoid Mary. People have tried to rehabilitate her image, including celebrity food writer Anthony Bourdain in his book *Typhoid Mary*, by pointing out the chef aspect to her personality. Judith Leavitt takes an academic approach to the question of healthy carriers and personal liberty in her book, *Typhoid Mary: Captive to the Public's Health*. Being human, we will always deal with outbreaks of infectious diseases, which is what makes her sad story so interesting. The CDC's website laid out the rules for quarantine, but, as Ebola showed us in 2013, even quarantine isn't so cut and dry.

Chapter Nine

There aren't many more famous gangsters than John Dillinger. Maybe that's why his life, although one of the more recent ones in this book, is shrouded in mystery. Everyone wanted to mythologize the brazen bank robber. His exploits snowballed even before his death. Tips and sightings came in from everyone and everywhere. It only got worse after his death. I used two historians' biographies to suss out the facts as I saw them. The FBI website has a huge dossier on him, as well as J. Edgar Hoover's fascination with the gangster. The Indiana State Police website proudly explains his contentious relationship with Captain Matt Leach.

Chapter Ten

Feisty Emmeline Pankhurst has always been polarizing. I read about her life from her own hand in her autobiography *My Own Story* and from a scholar's perspective in June Purvis's biography. The modern-day question of the hunger strike was addressed in an article on BBC, and the history of militant suffragists in general came from Laura E. Nym Mayhall's book.

Chapter Eleven

For such an amazing woman in American history, there aren't too many books on Virginia Hall. The most comprehensive one is by Judith L. Pearson, which recounts Hall's entire life. Information on women in the CIA and the sisterhood that took down Osama Bin Laden came from the CIA's website and the National Women's History Museum. There are more great books out there on OSS and SOE women operatives during World War II if you're interested in these courageous (and somewhat suicidal) women.

Chapter Twelve

What can be better than hearing about someone's life in his own words? Of course, to get at the story in between the lines, it's best to read multiple sources. I compared Nelson Mandela's autobiography with a biography written by Martin Meredith, an expert in South African history. A collection of essays in *The Cambridge Companion to Nelson Mandela* helped illuminate his fugitive months abroad, while *The Rise and Fall of Apartheid* revealed the dark side to the white minority in twentieth-century South Africa. A fascinating firsthand account of his presidential election came from *New York Times* reporter Bill Keller, who was in South Africa for the 1994 election and who was able to tag along on a typical day in office during Mandela's first year as president.

Sources

Chapter One

Crompton, Samuel Willard. *Julius Caesar*. Ancient World Leaders. New York: Chelsea House Publishers, 2003.

"Roman Gladiator." *Encyclopedia Romana*. Last modified 2015. Accessed February 12, 2015. http://penelope.uchicago.edu/~grout/encyclopaedia_romana/gladiators/gladiators.html.

Shaw, Brent D. *Spartacus and the Slave Wars*. Boston: Bedford/St. Martin, 2001.

Strauss, Barry. *The Spartacus War*. New York: Simon & Schuster, 2009.

Chapter Two

Burstein, Stanley M. *The Reign of Cleopatra*. Greenwood Guides to Historic Events of the Ancient World. Westport, CT: Greenwood Press, 2004.

Dio, Cassius. *Roman History*. Vol. 5. Cambridge, MA: Loeb Classical Library, 1917. Last accessed February 12, 2015. http://penelope.uchicago.edu/Thayer/E/Roman/Texts/Cassius_Dio/50*.html.

Erskine, Andrew. "Life after Death: Alexandria and the Body of Alexander." *Greece & Rome*, 2nd series, 49, no. 2 (October 2002): 163-79.

Fagan, Garret G. "Augustus." *An Online Encyclopedia of Roman Rulers*. Last modified July 2004. http://www.luc.edu/roman-emperors/auggie.htm.

Kleiner, Diane E. E. *Cleopatra and Rome*. Cambridge, MA: Belknap Press of Harvard University Press, 2005.

Lange, Carsten Hjort. "The Battle of Actium and the 'Slave of Passion.'" *Reinventing History: The Enlightenment Origins of Ancient History*. London: University of London, 2008: 115-136. Last accessed February 12, 2015. www.academia.edu/7442504/The_Battle_of_Actium_and_the_slave_of_passion.

Miles, Margaret M., ed. *Cleopatra: A Sphinx Revisited*. Berkeley, CA: University of California Press, 2011.

Roller, Duane W. *Cleopatra: A Biography*. Oxford, England: Oxford University Press, 2010.

Walker, Susan, and Sally Ashton. *Cleopatra*. Ancients in Action. London: Bristol Classical Press, 2006.

Chapter Three

Bainton, Roland H. *Here I Stand: A Life of Martin Luther*. Peabody, MA: Hendrickson Publishers, 1950.

Hendrix, Scott H. *Martin Luther: A Very Short Introduction*. Oxford: Oxford University Press, 2010.

Jones, Jim. "Background to *Against the Sale of Indulgences*." 2012. Accessed January 7, 2015. http://courses.wcupa.edu/jones/his101/web/37luther.htm.

Marty, Martin. *Martin Luther*. New York: Viking Press, 2004.

McKim, Donald K., ed. *The Cambridge Companion to Martin Luther*. Cambridge, MA: Cambridge University Press, 2003.

Sandberg, Brian. "HIST 414 European Wars of Religion." *Historical Perceptions*. Accessed July 18, 2014. http://briansandberg.wordpress.com/.

University of Texas at Austin. "Books Before and After the Gutenberg Bible." Harry Ransom Center. Accessed April 15, 2015. www.hrc.utexas.edu/educator/modules/gutenberg/books/.

Wilson, Derek. *Out of the Storm: The Life and Legacy of Martin Luther*. New York: St. Martin's Press, 2008.

Chapter Four

Andrade, Tonio. *Lost Colony: The Untold Story of China's First Great Victory over the West*. Princeton: Princeton University Press, 2011.

Anthony, Robert, J. *Like Froth Floating on the Sea: The World of Pirates and Sea-farers in Late Imperial South China*. Berkeley, CA: Institute of East Asian Studies, University of Berkeley, California, 2003.

Chen, Weichung. *War, Trade and Piracy in the China Seas (1622-1683)*. Leiden, The Netherlands: Koninklijke Brill NV, 2013.

Clements, Jonathan. *Coxinga and the fall of the Ming Dynasty*. Gloucestershire: The History Press, 2005.

Ko, Dorothy. *Teachers of the Inner Chambers: Women and Culture in Seventeenth-Century China*. Stanford, CA: Stanford University Press, 1994.

Ministry of Foreign Affairs. "Ming Koxinga Era." The Irresistible Charms of Taiwanese Architecture. Last accessed January 20, 2015. www.taiwan.gov.tw/ct.asp?xItem=37232&CtNode=2230&mp=13.

Parker, Geoffrey. *The Military Revolution: Military Innovation and the Rise of the West, 1500-1800*. Cambridge, MA: Cambridge University Press, 1988.

Spence, Jonathon. *The Search for Modern China*. New York: W.W. Norton, 1990.

Chapter Five

Ackroyd, Peter. *Tudors: The History of England from Henry VIII to Elizabeth I*. New York: St. Martin's Press, 2012.

BBC News (London). "Scottish Referendum: Scotland Votes 'No' to Independence." September 19, 2014. Accessed May 12, 2015. http://www.bbc.com/news/uk-scotland-29270441.

Massie, Allan. *The Royal Stuarts: A History of the Family that Shaped Britain*. New York: St. Martin's Press, 2010.

Meyer, G. J. *The Tudors: The Complete Story of England's Most Notorious Dynasty*. New York: Delacorte Press, 2012.

Porter, Linda. *Tudors versus Stewarts: The Fatal Inheritance of Mary, Queen of Scots*. New York: St. Martin's Press, 2013.

Sommerville, J. P. "Elizabeth I." University of Wisconsin: Madison. Last modified January 2015. Accessed May 12, 2015. http://faculty.history.wisc.edu/sommerville/361/361-14.htm.

Chapter Six

Bradford, William. *Of Plymouth Plantation*. 1647. Reprint. Gutenberg eBook, 2008.

Bunker, Nick. *Making Haste From Babylon: The Mayflower Pilgrims and Their World*. New York: Alfred Knopf, 2010.

Coffey, John. *Persecution and Toleration in Protestant England 1558-1689*. New York: Routledge, 2013.

Dunkerly, Robert. "Growth and Settlement beyond Jamestown." National Park Service. Last modified 1998. www.nps.gov/jame/historyculture/growth-and-settlement-beyond-jamestown.htm.

"The Early Colonial Trade in Furs." University of Massachusetts. Last accessed November 25, 2014. www.bio.umass.edu/biology/conn.river/furtrade.html.

"The 'First Thanksgiving' at Plymouth." Pilgrim Hall Museum. Last modified 2012. www.pilgrimhallmuseum.org/index.html.

Maxwell, Richard Howland. "Pilgrim and Puritan: A Delicate Distinction." *Pilgrim Society Notes*, 2nd series, March 2003.

"Religion and the Founding of the American Republic." Library of Congress. Last accessed November 24, 2014. www.loc.gov/exhibits/religion/rel01.html.

Schmidt, Gary D. *William Bradford: Plymouth's Faithful Pilgrim*. Grand Rapids, MI: Eerdmans Books for Young Readers, 1999.

Chapter Seven

Clinton, Catherine. *Harriet Tubman: The Road to Freedom*. New York: Little Brown and Company, 2004.

"Harriet Tubman's Role in Montgomery's Raids." University of North Florida. Last accessed April 9, 2015. www.unf.edu/floridahistoryonline/montgomery/tubman.html.

Humez, Jean M. *Harriet Tubman: The Life and Stories*. Madison, WI: University of Wisconsin Press, 2003.

Larson, Kate Clifford. *Bound for the Promised Land*. New York: One World Ballantine Books, 2004.

Sernett, Milton C. *Harriet Tubman: Myth, Memory, and History*. Durham, NC: Duke University Press, 2007.

Chapter Eight

Baker, S. Josephine. *Fighting for Life*. New York: New York Review of Books, 2013.

Bourdain, Anthony. *Typhoid Mary: An Urban Historical*. New York: Bloomsbury, 2001.

Leavitt, Judith Walzer. *Typhoid Mary: Captive to the Public's Health*. Boston: Beacon Press, 2006.

Loharikar, Anagha, et al. "Typhoid Fever Outbreak Associated with Frozen Mamey Pulp Imported from Guatemala to Western United States, 2010." *Clinical Infections Diseases*, July 1, 2012: 61-66.

Muhumuza, Rodney. "Ugandan Official: Typhoid Outbreak Infects Hundreds in the Capital, Likely to Spread." *US News and World Report*, March 25, 2015. Accessed April 3, 2015. www.usnews.com/news/world/articles/2015/03/25/ugandan-official-typhoid-sickens-hundreds-in-capital.

Porter, Nancy. *The Most Dangerous Woman in America*. Produced by Peter Frumkin. 2004. Boston: NOVA, 2004. DVD.

Powell, John. *Encyclopedia of North American Immigration*. New York: Facts on File, Inc., 2005.

"Quarantine and Isolation." Centers for Disease Control and Prevention. Last modified July 2014. www.cdc.gov/quarantine/.

The Richmond Planet. "Typhoid Mary Wants Liberty." Richmond, VA: July 10, 1909: 8. Digital File.

Soper, George A. "The Curious Case of Typhoid Mary." Bulletin of the New York Academy of Sciences, October 1939: 698-712.

Chapter Nine

Aronson, Marc. *Master of Deceit: J. Edgar Hoover and America in the Age of Lies*. Castleton, NY: Candlewick Press, 2012.

"A Byte out of History: Machine Gun Kelly and the Legend of the G-Men." Federal Bureau of Investigation. Last modified 2003. Last accessed February 25, 2015. www.fbi.gov/news/stories/2003/september/kelly092603.

Federal Bureau of Investigation. "John Dillinger." Famous Cases and Criminals. Accessed February 18, 2015. www.fbi.gov/about-us/history/famous-cases/john-dillinger.

Girardin, G. Russell and William J. Helmer. *Dillinger: The Untold Story*. Bloomington, IN: Indiana University Press, 1994.

Gorn, Elliot J. *Dillinger's Wild Ride: The Year that Made America's Public Enemy Number One*. Oxford: Oxford University Press, 2009.

Kennedy, Susan Estabrook. *The Banking Crisis of 1933*. Lexington, KY: University Press of Kentucky, 1973.

Matera, Dary. *John Dillinger: the Life and Death of America's First Celebrity Criminal*. New York: Avalon, 2004.

"The Pursuit of Public Enemy #1." Indiana State Police Department. Accessed February 21, 2015. www.in.gov/isp/2629.htm.

Chapter Ten

Bartley, Paula. *Emmeline Pankhurst*. London: Routledge, 2002.

Kohari, Alizeh. "Hunger Strikes: What Can They Achieve?" BBC. Last modified 2011. Accessed 2014. www.bbc.com/news/magazine-14540696.

Mayhall, Laura E. Nym. *The Militant Suffrage Movement: Citizenship and resistance in Britain, 1860-1930*. Oxford: Oxford University Press, 2003.

Pankhurst, Emmeline. *My Own Story*. 1914. Reprint, New York: Source Book Press, 1970.

Purvis, June. *Emmeline Pankhurst: A Biography*. London: Routledge, 2002.

Sadler, Victoria. "New Suffragettes Display at the National Portrait Gallery." *Huffington Post*. Last modified August 21, 2014. www.huffingtonpost.co.uk/victoria-sadler/new-suffragettes-national-portrait-gallery_b_5697155.html.

Chapter Eleven

Binney, Marcus. *The Women Who Lived for Danger: Agents of the Special Operations Executive*. New York: William Morrow, 2002.

McIntosh, Elizabeth P. *Women of the OSS: Sisterhood of Spies*. Annapolis, MD: Naval Institute Press, 1998.

Payment, Simone. *American Women Spies of World War II*. New York: The Rosen Publishing Group, Inc., 2004.

Pearson, Judith L. *The Wolves at the Door: The True Story of America's Greatest Female Spy*. Guilford, CT: The Lyons Press, 2005.

"Spotlight on the Sisterhood at the CIA." Central Intelligence Agency. Last modified March 2014. www.cia.gov/news-information/featured-story-archive/2014-featured-story-archive/spotlight-on-sisterhood-at-the-cia.html.

"Virginia Hall." NWHM.org. National Women's History Museum. Last accessed July 21, 2014. www.nwhm.org/education-resources/biography/biographies/virginia-hall/.

Windrem, Robert. "Sisterhood of Spies: Women Crack the Code at the CIA." National Broadcasting Corporation. Last accessed July 21, 2014. www.nbcnews.com/news/other/sisterhood-spies-women-crack-code-cia-f2D11594601.

Chapter Twelve

Barnard, Rita, ed. *Cambridge Companion to Nelson Mandela*. Cambridge, MA: Cambridge University Press, 2014.

Keller, Bill. *Tree Shaker: The Story of Nelson Mandela*. Boston: Kingfisher, 2008.

Mandela, Nelson. *A Long Walk to Freedom*. New York: Little, Brown and Company, 1995.

Meredith, Martin. *Mandela: A Biography*. New York: Public Affairs, 1997.

Michigan State University. "The End of Apartheid and the Birth of Democracy." *South Africa: Overcoming Apartheid Building Democracy*. Last accessed February 2, 2015. http://overcomingapartheid.msu.edu/unit.php?id=65-24E-6&page=1.

Sanders, David G. "Why Won't Mandela Renounce Violence?" *New York Times* (New York City, NY), June 21, 1990.

Welsh, David. *The Rise and fall of Apartheid*. Charlottesville, VA: University of Virginia Press, 2009.

Image Credits

Chapter One

Gladiator Mosaic 2nd–3rd century CE, courtesy of Wikimedia Commons Public Domain / Source: Romische Villa Nennig Museum via Dulcem in 2008

Roman Legionaries, courtesy of Wikimedia Commons / CC BY-SA 3.0 by author MatthiasKabel in 2005

Crassus and Spartacus Map, courtesy of Wikimedia Commons / CC BY-SA 3.0 by author Antoine Kerfant in 2007

Chapter Two

Tetradrachm of Marc Antony on obverse and Cleopatra on reverse, courtesy of Wikimedia Commons Public Domain / Source: British Museum via PHGCOM in 2009

Cleopatra before Caesar by Jean-Leon Gerome in 1866, courtesy of Wikimedia Commons Public Domain / Source: Private Collection via Dmitry Rozhkov in 2009

The Death of Julius Caesar by Vincenzo Camuccini in 1805, courtesy of Wikimedia Commons Public Domain / Source: Galleria Nazionale d'Arte Moderna via EfeX in 2005

Antony and Cleopatra by Lawrence Alma-Tadema in 1885, courtesy of Wikimedia Commons Public Domain / Source: Private Collection via Wmpearl in 2011

Map of the Battle of Actium, courtesy of Wikimedia Commons / CC BY-SA 3.0 by author Future Perfect at Sunrise in 2008

Augustus of Prima Porta at Museos Vaticanos in Rome, Italy, courtesy of Wikimedia Commons /CC BY-SA 3.0 by author Soerfm in 2013

Chapter Three

Catacomb Saint at St. Gallen in Wil, Switzerland, courtesy of Wikimedia Commons /CC BY-SA 3.0 by author Dbu in 2006

Satan Distributing Indulgences, courtesy of Wikimedia Commons Public Domain / Source: Illumination in a Czech Manuscript from 1490 via Packare in 2014

Luther Burning Papal Summons (iStock Illustration: 16681696; stock illustration © jpa1999)

Luther before the Diet of Worms by Anton von Werner in 1877, courtesy of Wikimedia Commons Public Domain / Source: Staatsgalerie Stuttgart via Vitold Muratov in 2010

Wartburg Room between 1890-1905, courtesy of Wikimedia Commons Public Domain / Source: Photochrom via Jan Arkesteijn in 2009

Katherine von Bora by Lucas Cranach the Elder in 1528, courtesy of Wikimedia Commons Public Domain / Source: Lower Saxony State Museum via Hajotthu in 2010

Chapter Four

Shunzhi Emperor by Anonymous Qing Court Painter, courtesy of Wikimedia Commons Public Domain / Source: Palace Museum, Beijing via Qingprof in 2011

The Kangxi Emperor on tour in the 18th century, courtesy of Wikimedia Commons Public Domain / Source: Palace Museum, Beijing via Louis le Grand in 2006

Taiwan-CIA Map, courtesy of Wikimedia Commons Public Domain / Source: Ras67 in 2011

Surrender of Fort Zeelandia in Formosa by Jan van Baden in 1675, courtesy of Wikimedia Commons Public Domain / Source: Neglected Formosa via Taiwantaffy in 2009

Koxinga Temple in Tainan, courtesy of Wikimedia Commons Public Domain / Source: Bcody80 in 2007

Chapter Five

Young Mary Stuart, courtesy of Wikipedia Commons Public Domain / Source: Lubomirski Museum via Kaho in 2013

Notre Dame de Paris, courtesy of Wikimedia Commons / CC BY-SA 3.0 by author DXR in 2014

Mary Stuart, James Darnley, courtesy of Wikipedia Commons Public Domain / Source: National Trust Collections via Kaho in 2008

Kirk o' Field Contemporary Sketch, courtesy of Wikipedia Commons Public Domain / Source: National Archives (UK) via Cactus.man in 2007

Loch Leven Castle (iStock Illustration: 59910290; stock photo © Rayban34)

Mary, Queen of Scots Escaping from Loch Leven Castle by William Craig Shirreff in 1805, courtesy of Wikipedia Commons Public Domain / Source: National Galleries of Scotland via Jonathan Oldenbuck in 2008

Mary's Cipher Code, courtesy of Wikipedia Commons Public Domain / Source: UK National Archives via Tomwhite56 in 2010

Chapter Six

The First Thanksgiving by Jean Leon Gerome Ferris in 1915, courtesy of Wikimedia Commons Public Domain / Source: Private Collection via Howcheng in 2010

Portrait of James I of England by Paul van Somer in 1620, courtesy of Wikimedia Commons Public Domain / Source: Royal Collection via Krinkle 2010

Title page from *A Treatise of the Ministry of the Church of England* published by William Brewster, courtesy of Wikimedia Commons Public Domain / Source: Collection of Yale University Library, photographed in 1899 via IMeowbot in 2006

Squanto Teaching the Colonists by The German Kali Works in 1911, courtesy of Wikimedia Commons Public Domain / Source: Bricker, Garland Armor. *The Teaching of Agriculture in the High School*. New York: Macmillan, 1911. Page 112

Chapter Seven

Harriet Tubman Reward Poster by Eliza Ann Brodress in Cambridge Democrat in 1849, courtesy of Wikipedia Commons Public Domain / Source: Cambridge Democrat via Scartol in 2007

Harriet Tubman Locations Map by Scartol, courtesy of Wikipedia Commons Public Domain / Source: Scartol in 2007

John Brown reproduction of daguerreotype by Martin M. Lawrence in 1859, courtesy of Wikipedia Commons Public Domain / Source: Library of Congress via Scewing in 2010

USS Cairo on Mississippi River in 1862, courtesy of Wikipedia Commons Public Domain / Source: U.S. Naval Historical Center via EraserGirl in 2008

Harriet Tubman photograph by H. Seymour Squyer in 1885, courtesy of Wikipedia Commons Public Domain / Source: National Portrait Gallery via Scewing in 2010

Harriet Tubman Home for the Aged photograph, courtesy of Wikipedia Commons Public Domain / Source: Lvklock in 2007

Chapter Eight

Mulberry Street, New York City by Anonymous Photographer in 1900 prepared by Detroit Photographic Co., courtesy of Wikipedia Commons Public Domain / Source: Library of Congress via Trialsanderrors in 2008

Mary Mallon Typhoid Poster in The New York American 1909, courtesy of
    Wikipedia Commons Public Domain / Source: via Ideru 2006

Mary Mallon in bed in The New York American 1909, courtesy of Wikipedia
    Commons Public Domain / Source: via Ideru 2006

North Brother Island, courtesy of Wikimedia Commons / CC BY-SA 3.0 by
    author Beyond My Ken in 2014

Chapter Nine

Food line at Yonge Street Mission, Toronto, Canada by Anonymous Photogra-
    pher in 1930s, courtesy of Wikipedia Commons Public Domain / Source:
    Yonge Street Mission via Skeezix1000 in 2007

John Dillinger Wanted Poster, courtesy of Wikipedia Commons Public Domain /
    Source: FBI via Jbarta in 2013

Biograph Theater by Anonymous Photographer in in Chicago 1934, courtesy
    of Wikipedia Commons Public Domain / Source: FBI via Gedas86 in 2009

Death Mask of John Dillinger at Museum of Crime and Punishment in Wash-
    ington, DC, courtesy of Wikimedia Commons / CC BY-SA 3.0 by author
    Jewelr07 in 2008

Chapter Ten

Portrait Badge of Emmeline Pankhurst circa 1909, courtesy of Wikipedia Com-
    mons Public Domain / Source: Museum of London via Magnus Manske
    in 2012

Passing of the Parliament Bill in the House of Lords by Sameul Begg in 1911,
    courtesy of Wikipedia Commons Public Domain / Source: *The Rise of
    Democracy* by Joseph Clayton via Tagishsimon in 2007

Emmeline Arrested by Anonymous Photographer in 1914, courtesy of Wiki-
    pedia Commons Public Domain / Source: Imperial War Museum via Fae
    in 2014

Suffragette Force fed, courtesy of Wikipedia Commons Public Domain /
    Source: Pankhurst, Sylvia. *The Suffragette*. New York: Sturgis & Walton
    Co, 1911. Page 433 Scartol in 2008

Suffragette that knew Jujitsu by Arthur Wallis Mills in 1910, courtesy of
   Wikipedia Commons Public Domain / Source: Punch Magazine via Mis-
   tress Selina Kyle in 2012

Chapter Eleven

France Map, courtesy of Wikimedia Commons / CC BY-SA 3.0 by author
   Rama in 2008

French Identification Certificate by Photographer Rudi Williams in 2002,
   courtesy of Wikipedia Commons Public Domain / Source: PD-USGOV via
   Nabak 2014

Virginia Hall receiving Distinguished Service Cross by Anonymous Photographer in 1945, courtesy of Wikipedia Commons Public Domain / Source:
   PD-USGOV in 2006

Chapter Twelve

Qunu by Salym Fayad Photographer in 2012, courtesy of Wikimedia Commons / CC BY-SA 2.0 by author Alifazal in 2013

Young Mandela by Anonymous Photographer in 1937, courtesy of Wikipedia
   Commons Public Domain / Source: www.anc.org via Fountain Posters in
   2014

Durban Sign by Anonymous Photographer in 1989, courtesy of Wikimedia
   Commons / CC BY-SA 2.0 by author Guinnog in 2008

Architects of Apartheid by Anonymous Photographer in unknown year, courtesy of Wikipedia Commons Public Domain / Source: Apartheid Museum
   Archives via Indech in 2005

Mandela's Prison Cell on Robben Island, courtesy of Wikimedia Commons /
   CC BY-SA 2.0 by author Witstinkhout in 2013

Index